DE[VON]
CORNWALL
Short Break Guide

THE WEST COUNTRY

FISHING PORTS

The principal industry in the past for this region was fishing, and numerous small seaports developed at almost every natural inlet, especially along the more sheltered south coast. The north coasts of both counties are generally more bleak and gale-lashed, with high cliffs, providing few opportunities to develop ports.

Pilchards and mackerel were the main catch and almost everyone in the villages that grew up around these small harbours was engaged in the industry in some way. Sadly, the fishing fleets are now much depleted, and most ports have turned to tourism as their main industry. Some fishermen have managed to combine the two and use their craft to take tourists on game fishing trips for such exotic prey as sharks, quite prevalent in the seas off south-west England.

The West Country comprises Devon and Cornwall. It is a very distinctive and beautiful region, famous for its spectacular coastline, seafaring, remote villages, beautiful gardens, intimate country lanes, mysterious legends, wild moorland scenery, time-shattered ruins - and cream teas! It is an area of great contrasts, offering the visitor every conceivable form of entertainment and attraction. The southern coasts of Devon and Cornwall have often been referred to as the 'English Riviera'. But this is no fanciful title dreamed up by the tourist industry; the deep blue sea, vivid skies, whitewashed buildings and fine sands really do conjure up images of the Mediterranean.

CLIMATE

The Southwest region enjoys the mildest and most equable climate in Britain. In parts of Cornwall and South Devon, even subtropical plants are able to flourish in the comparatively warm, moist air, virtually free of winter frosts. Unfortunately, as well as being one of the sunniest parts of Britain, with long hours of sunshine recorded, it is also one of the wettest. Neither is all quite as idyllic as it might seem, for in winter the Atlantic coasts are often battered by hurricane-force winds.

A BRIEF BACKGROUND TO THE REGION

DARTMOOR

Dartmoor is the largest tract of truly wild open countryside left in the south of England. A prelude to the mountains of Wales and Cumbria beyond, Dartmoor is believed to be the granite core of a mountain, long-since eroded away, that many millions of years ago may have been higher than Everest. The moor today contains a breathtaking mixture of scenery, ranging from forests with fast-flowing streams to bleak heathland, punctuated by distinctive rock stacks, known as tors (shown above).

LAND APART

Until the coming of the railway, Cornwall really was a land apart, a virtual island, separated from the rest of England by the River Tamar. Before the famous Victorian engineer Isambard Kingdom Brunel built his railway bridge across the Tamar at Saltash (shown here) in 1859, opening up this remote corner of Britain, Cornwall was regarded almost as a separate kingdom. The people, like those of Wales, are of Celtic descent, with their own special dialect and language, virtually unspoken now, but still recognisable in the curious place-names. Similarly, the name for Devon comes from a Celtic word meaning 'land of deep valleys'.

INDUSTRIAL PAST

The Cornish countryside is littered with remnants of its industrial past. After fishing, the main industry has always been mineral extraction. In ancient times both gold and silver were mined, but by far the most common form of mining was for tin. First extracted about 4,000 years ago, it was alloyed with copper to produce bronze. Tin was mined throughout the Roman and medieval periods, but enjoyed fluctuating success. As the more accessible seams became worked out, so it became necessary to mine more deeply into the rock, shafts often extending far out to sea. During the 18th and 19th centuries, tin mining flourished, thanks largely to the invention of steam engines, developed by the Cornish engineer Richard Trevithick, which pumped flood water from the deep mines and drove the machinery. (Trevithick's statue, shown here, can be seen at Camborne, his birthplace.) The most familiar relics of the tin industry are the deserted engine houses, built to house the enormous steam engines and pumps, such as the one shown above at Wheal Coates, now a National Trust property and freely accessible from the cliff path near St. Agnes.

FAVOURITE BEACHES

Without doubt, Cornwall possesses some of the finest beaches and coastal scenery to be found anywhere in the British Isles. Coupled with a mild climate and blue seas, this area is idyllic. Facilities generally are good, with some of the cleanest beaches in the country.

1 NEWQUAY

Newquay is Cornwall's largest and most popular holiday resort, boasting several fine sandy beaches on the north, Atlantic coast. The area has become popular with surfers (world championship events are regularly held there) and the rollers are reckoned to be the third best in the world after Hawaii and Australia.

P ⛽ WC ♿ 🚂 - Newquay

8 ST. IVES

The picturesque and bustling little town of St. Ives has become one of Cornwall's leading resorts, popular with surfers and families. Once a busy fishing port, the town became popular with artists in the 19th century (as it still is) because of the clarity of the light there. There are several sandy beaches, all easily accessible from the town.

P ⛽ WC ♿ 🚂 - St. Ives

7 PORTHCURNO

The sheer beauty of this fine, sandy beach when viewed from the cliff path above has to be seen to be believed. Overlooked by the unique Minack Theatre (see page 18), it is a truly magnificent setting on the Land's End peninsula. The trans-Atlantic telephone cable comes ashore on this beach. In the cliffs at the head of the beach is a curious 'house' carved out of solid rock.

P ⛽ WC ♿ 🚂 - Penzance

6 MULLION COVE

This beautiful cove, on the Lizard Peninsula, enjoys one of the mildest climates in Britain. Dramatically sited between immense and towering cliffs, it was once a popular haunt of smugglers. Contraband was often tied to rocks and sunk until it could be safely brought ashore. There is a small harbour and several small sandy beaches at Mullion and just north at Polurrian Cove.

P WC 🚂 - Falmouth

CORNWALL

2 BEDRUTHAN STEPS

Situated between Newquay and Padstow on Cornwall's Atlantic, northern coast, the sandy beach at Bedruthan Steps sits beneath towering granite cliffs, owned, like so many stretches of the coast here, by the National Trust. The curious name is said to derive from a giant, named Bedruthan, who hurled the rocks into the sea and used them as stepping stones. The steps leading down to the beach were said to have been cut by wreckers.

> *i* It is worth contacting the relevant TIC for full disabled facilities. Facilities generally are good, with some of the cleanest waters in Europe.

3 GORRAN HAVEN

Just a few miles down the road from Mevagissey, the charming, though less picturesque, village of Gorran Haven has two fine sandy beaches. One of them is only accessible at low tide or by negotiating a steep flight of steps leading down from a footpath. There are many rocks strewn across the beach and several caves that provide adventure for children.

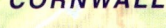

> *i* Because of the often rugged terrain, access to many Cornish beaches is difficult for disabled people. Sometimes, access is only possible by steps.

4 PENDOWER

Pendower is a world apart from the hustle and bustle of the quaint village of Mevagissey being, a real haven of peace and quiet. Accessible only by two narrow roads that do not quite meet (thus preventing through traffic), refreshment facilities are provided by a hotel situated right on the sands of the beach itself, the most romantic of locations.

5 KYNANCE COVE

Kynance Cove possesses some of the most beautiful and spectacular beaches and coastal scenery anywhere. The rocks are serpentine (greenish) in colour and the sea a vivid blue. It has been said that Kynance is more like Greece than Greece itself, so Mediterranean is the atmosphere. There are several sandy beaches here (reached by steep steps) and a number of curiously named rocks.

6 FAVOURITE BEACHES

The beaches of Devon are very similar to those of Cornwall. The north coast is windier, exposed to the Atlantic rollers and popular with surfers. The south coast is altogether different in character, with quiet coves and sheltered, sandy bays. Facilities are generally very good, with safe bathing.

9 BIGBURY-ON-SEA

An attractive small holiday resort, standing on low cliffs with a fine sandy beach. Just offshore is Burgh Island, which can be reached on foot at low tide. At high tide a tractor and trailer gives access. The more energetic can enjoy walks around the Avon estuary at low tide.

 - Ivybridge

16 SOAR MILL COVE

For the more energetic, the delightful beach at Soar Mill Cove is a few minutes walk from the car park in the village of Soar. Surrounded by low cliffs, the beach is crossed by streams and dotted with rock pools at low tide.

in Soar village, limited facilities - Totnes

15 SOUTH SANDS & NORTH SANDS

These two beautiful beaches are within easy reach of Salcombe, on the south Devon coast. South Sands stands at the end of a wooded valley that is overlooked by the sub-tropical gardens of Sharpitor.

 - Totnes

ℹ Coastguard

In an emergency, telephone 999 and ask for the Coastguard Service. Give clear, concise details to the operator. Do not use the emergency service to request information - contact the relevant Tourist Information Centre (see pages 42-43).

14 SLAPTON SANDS

In the centre of Start Bay, southwest of Dartmouth, can be found Slapton Sands - slightly mis-named because the beach is a mixture of sand and shingle. The attraction here is a granite monument presented to the village by the United States army. In 1944, the residents evacuated their homes to enable the top-secret plans for the D-Day landings to be practised by the Allied forces. The monument is even more poignant because of the recent release of wartime documents that revealed a heavy loss of life during these manoeuvres. Inland, beyond a shingle ridge, is a large lake, Slapton Ley, the haunt of many species of wild fowl. Slapton village itself, just inland, is very pretty.

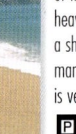

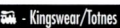 - Kingswear/Totnes

DEVON

10 WOOLACOMBE

Woolacombe is a small resort on the north Devon coast with several miles of wide, sandy beaches. Behind the beach rises the steep Woolacombe Down, a series of gorse-covered hills. The beach is pounded by the Atlantic rollers and is a favourite haunt of surfers. Further south, the Downs give way to rocky cliffs, with many sheltered coves.

P WC †◯¦ ♿ - Barnstaple

11 EXMOUTH - SANDY BAY

To the east of Exmouth lies a huge and sprawling holiday camp known as Sandy Bay nestling behind a beach. The beach is protected by towering, red sandstone cliffs and is a veritable sun-trap with good bathing. Day visitors are welcome and there is a huge car park above the beach.

P WC †◯¦
🚂 - Exmouth

The West Country affords some of the cleanest beaches, not only in Britain, but in Europe. The beaches are generally safe, but there may be dangerous undercurrents in certain areas, especially on the northern, Atlantic coast.

12 BEER

The familiar red sandstone cliffs of the southwestern Devon coast give way to chalk near Beer, a delightful, unspoilt fishing village that still manages to earn a living from the sea, despite having no harbour. The beach here is shingle, but its sheltered location makes it popular with holidaymakers. Rowing boats and motor launches can be hired. Beer was once a favourite haunt of smugglers. Modern attractions include a model railway and a miniature railway.

P WC ♿ †◯¦   🚂 - Axminster

Because of the difficult terrain, access for the disabled is sometimes limited. Always observe local lifeguard information and swim between any flags flying.

13 BLACKPOOL SANDS

Blackpool Sands, near Dartmouth, form a delightful bay, surrounded by pine-clad cliffs. Rhododendrons bloom in the early summer, giving the beach an exotic, almost Mediterranean feel. The beach here is a mixture of sand and fine, golden shingle, but it shelves steeply, so bathers should be careful. It forms part of a private estate. Windsurfing boards, water skis and floats can all be hired.

P WC †◯¦   🚂 - Kingswear/Totnes

CHILDREN'S DAYS OUT

The following selection of places to visit have been specially chosen with children in mind, to provide that extra bit of excitement. They range from family days out at leisure complexes, to wildlife parks and heritage centres, offering hands-on experiences to fuel their imaginations.

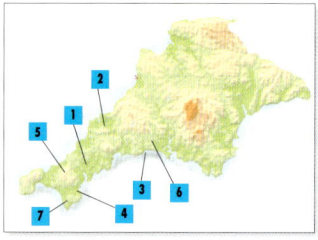

1 CALLESTOCK CIDER FARM

Off the A3075, Newquay Rd, Penhallow

The Callestock Cider Farm at Penhallow has something for all the family. See how real farm cider, country wines, jams and chutneys are made. There is also a museum of old tradesmen's tools and farming equipment, so you can compare the cider-making process of today with that of times gone by. For the children there is a traditional farmyard with animals, and a tractor and trailer ride through the orchards. Free samples of all products are available for tasting in the shop and delicious cream teas are served in the 'Piggery' café. Open daily, Feb.-mid-Dec. 01872 573356

P WC 🍴 ♿ 🚂 - Truro

2 DONKEY SANCTUARY

Lower Maidenland, St. Kew Highway, Wadebridge

This charming donkey sanctuary (known as N.E.D.D.I. - the New European Distressed Donkey Initiative Ltd.) is run on a non-profit-making basis with the sole objective to rescue and care for donkeys (and ponies) suffering from neglect or cruelty or threatened with slaughter - and to educate governments and individuals around the world to promote greater responsibility towards donkeys. Children will find this both an enjoyable and educational experience. Open daily Easter-Oct. (limited opening other times). 01208 841710

P WC 🍴 ♿ 🚂 - Bodmin Parkway

3 MONKEY SANCTUARY

Murrayton, near Looe

An unusual attraction, and one sure to be a great favourite with the children, is the Monkey Sanctuary at Murrayton, just east of Looe. The sanctuary is home to a protected colony of Amazonian Woolly monkeys, housed in large enclosures and

set in delightful grounds, high on the cliffs. Open March-Sept., Sun.-Thurs.

P WC 🍴 ♿ 🚂 - Looe

CORNWALL

4 NATIONAL SEAL SANCTUARY
Off the B3293, Gweek

Every year, the National Seal Sanctuary rescues and releases over 30 injured or abandoned seal pups. The sanctuary is also home to resident seals and sea lions that are unable to be returned to the wild. Set in 40 acres on the beautiful Helford Estuary, there is also a play area, quiz trail, picnic area, friendly farm animals and woodland walks. Open daily all year, except Christmas Day. 01326 221874

P WC †©† & 🚂 - Redruth/Falmouth

5 ST. AGNES LEISURE PARK
On the B3277, South of St. Agnes

Formerly a tin-mining village on Cornwall's north coast, there are many industrial reminders on the cliffs hereabouts. A little way outside the village can be found the St. Agnes Leisure Park. There are many rides and other attractions set within colourful landscaped gardens, including a fine model village, with miniature versions of many Cornish features. The nearby beach at Chapel Porth is excellent for bathing. Open daily. 01872 552793

P WC †©† & 🚂 - Truro/Redruth

6 DOBWALLS THEME PARK
Off the A38, East of Liskeard

To the west of Liskeard is Dobwalls Theme Park, one of Cornwall's premier amusement parks. New rides and attractions are constantly being added to meet the ever-increasing demand for excitement. Firm favourites include the Forest Railroad, with authentic American scenery and Mr. Thorburn's

Edwardian Countryside, where wildlife paintings are displayed in unique period settings.
Open various times, Mar.-Oct.
01579 320325.

P WC †©† & 🚂 - Liskeard

7 FLAMBARDS
Culdrose Manor, Helston

Flambards is one of Cornwall's top attractions. An all-weather family leisure park with internationally acclaimed exhibitions, rides (from the gentle to the daring), shows, live entertainment, award-winning gardens, a walk through a Victorian village with houses and shop displays, plus a life-like recreation of 'Britain in the Blitz'. There is something to cover all tastes here and for all ages. Flambards prides itself on its excellent facilities for the disabled and has even made provision for visitors to walk and water their dogs!
Open daily, Easter-Oct.
01326 564093

P WC &

🚂 - Redruth

🚂 - Falmouth

Children's Days Out

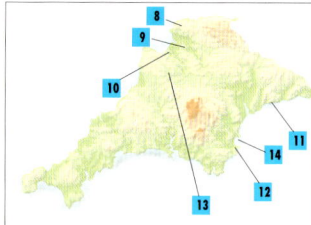

8 WILDLIFE & DINOSAUR PARK

Off the A399, Combe Martin, Ilfracombe

Step back in time at the Combe Martin Wildlife & Dinosaur Park and explore over 30 acres of subtropical gardens amid streams and cascading waterfalls, complete with life-size animated dinosaurs. There are also over 250 species of animals and rare and exotic plants as well as falconry displays, animal-handling sessions, an Earthquake Canyon train ride and a dinosaur museum. Open daily, Easter-Nov. 📞 01271 882486

P WC 🍴 ♿ 🚂 - Barnstaple

9 EXMOOR STEAM RAILWAY

On the A399, between Blackmoor Gate and Brayford

This is truly a family business, for everything at the Exmoor Steam Railway (including the locomotives, rolling stock, buildings, tracks and gardens) was built by members of the Stirland family. The two mile journey, through lovely grounds, takes about 25 minutes, but you can travel as many times as you wish during the day. The trains are all steam-operated and the carriages fully glazed. At almost 1,000ft. above sea level, it is the highest narrow gauge railway in England.
Open various times, Mar.-Oct. 📞 01598 710711

P WC 🍴 ♿ 🚂 - Barnstaple

10 THE BIG SHEEP

On the A39, North Devon Link Road, Bideford

'Open farm turned "wacky" tourist attraction' is how this award-winning Park bills itself! A great family day out in the country with hilarious novelties, like sheep racing and duck trials. On a more serious level are traditional rural crafts, such as sheepdog trials, cheese-making and everything else to do with sheep. There are also numerous live shows, a knitwear shop and delicious home cooking.
Open daily, all year. 📞 01237 477916

P WC 🍴 ♿ 🚂 - Barnstaple

DEVON

11 PECORAMA

Underleys, Beer

Pecorama is a railway themed attraction, set amidst glorious gardens and with many children's entertainments laid on. There is a mile-long light railway and a model railway. There is always an extensive programme of live

entertainment for the children, under cover, including clowns, magicians and jesters, crazy golf and several outdoor activity areas. The 'Peco Millennium Garden' is a new innovative garden project. Senior citizens and able-bodied helpers for wheelchair users are admitted free. Open daily, Easter-Sept.

☎ 01297 21542

P WC ⑩ ♿ 🚂 - Axminster

12 PAIGNTON ZOO

Totnes Road, Paignton

Paignton Zoo is one of the largest in Britain, housed in beautiful wooded grounds and formal gardens. Like many zoos now, it is more concerned with conservation and breeding endangered species than in simply exhibiting animals. There are many special features here, ideal for the children to learn about the wildlife, coupled with play areas where they can let off steam.
Open daily all year, except Christmas Day.

☎ 01803 527936

P WC ⑩ ♿ 🚂 - Paignton

13 DARTINGTON CRYSTAL

Linden Close, Great Torrington

If you are looking for an unusual day out for the children, why not take them round a working factory! They will be fascinated by the demonstration of glass-blowing techniques. Dartington Crystal is one of the West Country's leading attractions, with over 300,000 visitors a year, who come to watch skilled craftsmen create beautiful wares of crystal. There is a visitor centre, an exhibition and a factory shop, selling goods at low prices.
Open daily, all year. ☎ 01805 626269

P WC ⑩ ♿ 🚂 - Barnstaple

14 BYGONES

Fore Street, St. Mary Church, Torquay

'Bygones' used to be a cinema, so the building is much bigger than it appears from the outside. Inside is a life-sized reconstruction of a Victorian street, complete with shops, reconstructed period rooms and Fantasy Land, a world in miniature. Climb aboard the footplate of a real steam-engine and walk through a World War I trench and experience the sights, sounds and smells of life in the trenches.

Open daily at various times all year, except Christmas Day.

☎ 01803 326108

P (200 yards) WC ⑩ ♿

🚂 - Torquay

RAINY DAYS

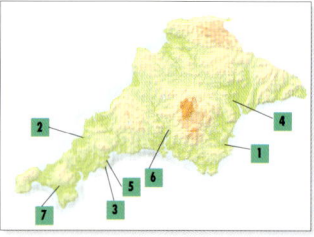

With so many of the West Country's attractions situated out of doors, what happens if it rains? Fortunately, there's no shortage of things to do, and here you'll find plenty of suggestions for places which are ideal to visit on a wet, grey day, although they are also worth seeing at any other time.

1 KENT'S CAVERN

Ilsham Road, Torquay

Kent's Cavern is one of several large show caves along this stretch of coast (there is another at nearby Brixham) which show signs of early habitation by man. Situated about 1 mile (1.5 km) east of the harbour, the skull of a sabre-toothed tiger has also been found there. The cave is regularly on show through the season and many of the finds discovered there can be seen at Torquay Museum. Open daily. 01803 215136

P WC ❯ (nearby)   🚂 - Torquay

2 SEA LIFE CENTRE

Towan Promenade, Newquay

Set on the Towan Bay promenade at Newquay, the Sea Life Centre is the ideal place to visit, even on rainy days. The centre is home to a variety of marine life, much of it found in Cornish waters. Special features are an underwater walk-through tunnel, enabling you to see sharks at close range, Kingdom of the Seahorse, touch-screen computers and CD-ROM programmes. You can enjoy a quiz or even touch some of the animals. Multi-level viewing brings the ocean floor vividly to life. Open all year (weekends only, Nov.-Feb.). 01637 87822

P WC ❯ ♿   🚂 - Newquay

3 WORLD OF MODEL RAILWAYS

Meadow Street, Mevagissey

Welcome to the fascinating miniature world of model railways. This is one of the finest private collections in the country, with extensive scenery backdrops and over 40 trains running in sequence, all under cover. There is something to see for all levels of interest, including a token-operated children's layout. Previously featured on both BBC and ITV television programmes. Open daily, Mar.- Oct. (Sun. only in winter). 01726 842457

P WC ❯ (in Mevagissey itself)

🚂 - St. Austell

CORNWALL & DEVON

4 EXETER UNDERGROUND TUNNELS

The Royal Albert Memorial Museum & Art Gallery, Queen Street, Exeter (access near Boot shop, in the High Street)

The Royal Albert Memorial Museum & Art Gallery is in itself an excellent place to visit, but it has an extra very unusual exhibit. Beneath the city is a network of medieval passageways, built in the 13th century to bring a clean water supply into the city. It is the only such system of passages that can be explored by the public in Britain. The visit includes a small museum, a video display and a guided tour. Not suitable for the severely disabled. Open Tues.-Sat. (Mon.-Sat. Jul.-Aug). 01392 265858

P WC ⑩ - town centre.   🚂 - Exeter

5 ST. AUSTELL BREWERY - VISITOR CENTRE

Trevorthian Road, St. Austell

St. Austell Brewery is Cornwall's oldest independent family brewery serving a range of traditional specialist beers at over 150 inns (several offering accommodation) throughout Devon and Cornwall. There are guided tours of the brewery, tracing the brewing process from start to finish, followed by a demonstration of wooden barrel-making by a cooper. Open Mon.-Fri. all year, except Christmas Day and Bank Holidays. 01726 66022

P WC ⑩ ♿   🚂 - St. Austell

6 MORWELLHAM QUAY, TAVISTOCK

Off the A390, near Tavistock

This is an exciting project designed to interpret and display the long 1,000-year history of this river port on the River Tamar. There is a great deal to see here, much

of it under cover, including an underground train ride into the historic copper mine, horse drawn carriages, workshops, cottages, demonstrations and a wildlife reserve. Visitors can even try on period costumes. Open daily all year, except 23 Dec-3 Jan inclusive. 01822 833808

P WC ⑩ ♿ (some)   🚂 - Gunnislake

7 POLDARK MINE, WENDRON

Off the B3297, at Wendron

Poldark Mine is a genuine Cornish tin mine. Visitors can don a plastic safety helmet and actually walk down the mine shafts. The mine was begun in the 1720s and has five shafts at three different levels. It was worked by man- and animal-power only, as it closed before the advent of steam engines. It has been open to the public since 1971 and now contains a museum and heritage centre, steam-pumping engines and a host of other attractions, including a play area and an amusement arcade. Open daily, Easter-Oct.

01326 573173

P WC ⑩ ♿

🚂 - Falmouth

THE FIRST CONVENIENCE FOOD

Originally, Cornish pasties provided a meal in themselves for farm and mine workers. They were made with thick short-crust pastry which had a ridged seal along the curved side. As the labourers could seldom get to a tap to wash their hands, they held the pastry by the thick, crusty ridge which they threw away after eating their meal. At one end was the dinner, while at the other was the dessert, such as jam pudding.

14 DAYS OF ADVENTURE

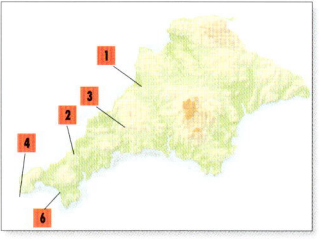

While for many the idea of a holiday is to relax, sit on a beach or around a hotel pool and sip cocktails, for others it is to take part in some form of activity. Some like to try something completely different or visit unusual places. If this sounds like you, then the suggestions on the following four pages should appeal. Here you will find a good range of unusual or challenging activities to choose from to add extra excitement to your visit.

1 WINDSURFING

Surf boards are available for hire (or purchase) at several beach site outlets, such as Bude, Newquay and St. Ives, if you fancy riding the waves. (Newcomers to the sport are advised to receive some instruction first, as the Atlantic rollers are more powerful than they look.) For those who prefer windsurfing, why not try one of the recognised centres, such as 'Outdoor Adventure' at Bude, who offer board hire and full training if needed. Outdoor Adventure, Atlantic Court, Widemouth Bay, Bude.

📞 01288 361312   🚂 - Barnstaple

2 WHEAL COATES MINE

Accessible from Chapel Porth Beach, St. Agnes

The beach and cliffs at Chapel Porth, near St. Agnes, are owned by the National Trust. From the beach a path climbs its way northwards along the cliff edge, leading to the ruined buildings of the Wheal Coates tin mine. The buildings, including the impressive remains of the engine house, have been restored by the National Trust and can be freely inspected at any time.

🅿 🚻 🍴 - at Chapel Porth Beach.

🚂 - Redruth/Truro

3 BODMIN MOOR

Often regarded as the poor relation to Dartmoor, Bodmin is much smaller (about 100 sq. miles/259

sq. km.), but in certain respects is bleaker and wilder. The moor is littered with prehistoric remains, and has close associations with King Arthur. Visitors are advised to purchase O.S. maps before crossing the wildest parts of the moor. An excellent way of seeing the moor is to take a train on the Bodmin Steam Railway which you can pick up at Bodmin, or at Bodmin Parkway on the A38.

🚂 - Bodmin Parkway

CORNWALL

4 LAND'S END

Sennen, Penwith Peninsula

The tourist magnet of Cornwall is undoubtedly Land's End, the most westerly point in England and some 874 miles (1,406 km) from John o' Groats in the far northeast of Scotland. There is now a large visitor attraction at Land's End with several award-winning museums and audio-visual displays, including the 'Last Labyrinth', the 'Relentless Sea' and 'Air Sea Rescue Alert'. There is also a farm, a hotel and several places to eat. Access to the conservation site, away from the attractions, is free (except for

car-parking), with individual charges for each attraction. Despite the sheer number of visitors, the dramatic scenery is awe-inspiring, and is still a place for quiet reflection, where Britain's mainland ends in spectacular fashion.
Open daily throughout the year, except Christmas Day. 01736 871501

P 🏠 🍴 ♿ 🚂 - Penzance

5 BOAT TRIPS

No visit to Cornwall would be complete without a boat trip, whether it be a fishing expedition, perhaps to catch sharks that swim in the warm waters just offshore, or a leisurely tour around the harbour. There is no better way to see Cornwall's spectacular coastline than from a boat. The best way to book your trip is direct, with the boat owners themselves, by walking along the harbour-side and reading the display boards. The following harbours regularly have boat excursions available:
Mevagissey, Town Quay; Fowey, Town Quay; Looe (to St. George's Island); Newquay (harbour trips); Penzance, North Pier (day trips to the Isles of Scilly); Falmouth, Prince of Wales Pier (or contact the nearest Tourist Information Centre if you want to book ahead - see page 43).

6 CULDROSE ROYAL NAVAL AIR STATION

On the A3083, near Helston

For air enthusiasts there is a public viewing area at the Culdrose Royal Naval Air Station, near Helston. Various military aircraft can regularly be seen here or flying in this area.

P 🚂 - Camborne/Falmouth

16 DAYS OF ADVENTURE

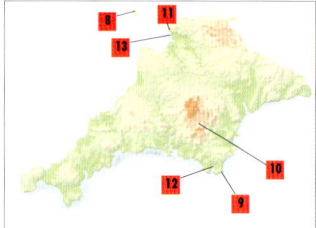

DARTMOOR PONIES

In Britain there are nine recognised breeds of pony, several of which have been allowed to roam free over large tracts of open land, living in an almost wild state in large herds. One of the more common of these is the Dartmoor pony, a sturdy animal standing about 12 hands high (about 4 ft/1 m) to the shoulder. Once used as pack-horses, they are now more likely to be encountered running free on the vast open spaces of Dartmoor, giving the moor a true sense of wildness.

7 BALLOON TRIPS

One of the most unusual and exhilarating ways to see the countryside is from a hot-air balloon. There is something quite magical about the experience of drifting silently (most of the time!) across the land at little more than walking pace; an experience never to be forgotten. Balloon trips are usually made in early morning, or evening, to take advantage of the thermals, and you never quite know where you will end up! Several companies operate trips in the West Country, including Exeter Balloons. ☎ 01404 823102

8 LUNDY ISLAND - OFF ILFRACOMBE

A definite must for all those who enjoy islands is Lundy, lying 24 miles (39 km) offshore in the Bristol Channel. The island measures about 3 miles (5 km) long by about half-a-mile (0.8 km) wide, with cliffs soaring up to 500 ft (152 m) high in places. It has a long history and contains the remains of a prehistoric settlement and a medieval castle. Once privately owned (the manor house is now a small hotel), the island is now owned by the National Trust, and is a bird-watcher's paradise. A small number of visitors can stay on the island, but most choose a day trip from Ilfracombe (several boats operate from the harbour).

For more information contact the local Tourist Information Centre ☎ 01271 863001.

WC 🍴 🚂 - Barnstaple

9 HALLSANDS, RUINED VILLAGE

On the Southern tip of Devon, just north of Stuart Point, is Hallsands. A walk along the beach at Hallsands can be a grim reminder of the awesome power of the sea. Towards the end of the 19th century, thousands of tons of shingle were removed from the beach here to build new docks at Devonport. Deprived of its natural defences, the village of Hallsands was swept away in a severe storm in 1917. The ruined cottages can still be seen at

the foot of the cliffs, a sad and enigmatic epitaph to a once thriving fishing community. Accessible any time from the beach.

P at top of cliff. 🚂 - Totnes

Devon

10 DARTMOOR

Dartmoor is one of Britain's premier National Parks and the largest tract of open countryside in Southern England. At 2,038 ft (620 m), it is also the highest region south of the Pennines. There are over 200 distinctive rocky summits, known as tors, rising from the moorland-like miniature mountains. Once away from the main tourist areas, the scenery is truly wild; ideal walking, climbing and pony trekking country. Visitors who intend straying off the beaten track should wear suitable clothing

and arm themselves with the appropriate O.S. maps. Contact Dartmoor National Park
📞 01822 890414
🚂 - Okehampton/Plymouth

11 PONY TREKKING

Devon affords many opportunities for pony trekking, in addition to the obvious attractions of Exmoor and Dartmoor. Roylands Riding Stables at Croyde Bay (B.H.S. approved) offer a range of treks, from novice to experienced level, lasting for 1 hour or longer, over a variety of glorious Devon scenery, from woodland to beach rides.
📞 01271 890898
P WC 🚂 - Barnstaple

12 OUTDOOR ADVENTURE

While some like to relax on holiday and let the world go by, others prefer to partake in exhilarating and challenging sports and activities to charge their batteries. Courtlands Adventure Centre, at Kingsbridge, offers a range of activities to fit the bill, whatever their interests, including sailing, water-skiing and windsurfing. 📞 01548 550227
P WC 🍴 ♿   🚂 - Totnes

13 CASCADES FAMILY ADVENTURE POOL

Cascades offers a great day out for the family, whatever the weather, including Tropical Adventure Pool, the Big Blue flume ride, a Rapids Ride and a toddlers' pool, all in a highly imaginative setting. There are also baby-changing facilities and late-night swimming sessions.
Open daily, Mar.-Oct.
📞 01271 820884
P WC 🍴 ♿
🚂 - Barnstaple

Hidden Delights

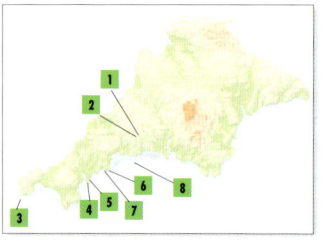

With the ever-increasing popularity of the West Country as a holiday destination, it is becoming more and more difficult to find any corner that is truly hidden. Amazingly, however, despite the heavy numbers of visitors, the region still retains its distinctive character and remains largely unspoilt. Although some of the places featured in this section are generally well visited, each still has hidden corners that never fail to delight and are well worth exploring.

1 THE CHEESEWRING

Located in the southeastern corner of Bodmin Moor and close to St. Cleer, can be found The Cheesewring, a curious natural rock formation, standing on the edge of a granite quarry over 1,000 ft (304 m) above sea level. The nearby hamlet of Minions lays claim to having the highest pub in Cornwall. Just west can be seen the Hurlers, three stone circles dating from the Bronze Age.

P ❙❙ - at Minions   🚂 - Liskeard

2 GOLITHA FALLS, ST. CLEER

On the southeastern fringes of Bodmin Moor can be found Golitha Falls, a series of beautiful cascades on the River Fowey. They are reached by turning north at Redgate, crossing an ancient packhorse bridge and following a footpath along wooded banks of the river. In the vicinity of St. Cleer can also be seen a Neolithic chamber tomb known as Trethevy Quoit, and a curious granite memorial stone dedicated to the Cornish King Doniert. (Note, it is advisable to equip yourself with the relevant O.S. map before attempting to explore this area, to prevent getting lost.)

P 🚂 - Liskeard

3 MINACK THEATRE

The setting for the Minack Open-Air Theatre on the cliff-tops above Porthcurno beach is truly breathtaking. Modelled on Greek amphitheatres, the theatre is the equal of anything to be seen in Greece. It was built in 1923, the creation of Miss Rowena Cade. Performances are staged throughout the season, and when not in use the theatre is open to day visitors. Accessible from the South Cornwall Coast Path or from a narrow side road near Porthcurno village.

📞 01736 810181

P WC ❙❙   🚂 - Penzance

CORNWALL

4 ROSELAND PENINSULA

The Roseland Peninsula is a small area lying between Carrick Roads and Gerrans Bay, just east of Falmouth. It is an area of outstanding natural beauty, quiet roads and spectacular coastline.

5 VERYAN

A delightful village on the Roseland Peninsula, Veryan sits snugly in a deep, wooded hollow. Nearby is the beautiful Pendower Beach, notable for having a hotel situated right on the beach (see pages 4-5). Veryan itself is famous for its round houses, charming two-storey white-washed houses with thatched roofs, each surmounted by a cross. They were built in the 19th century to ward off the devil; an old tradition states that the devil likes to lie in wait in corners inside houses, so those in Veryan gave him no place to hide!

P & 🚂 - Truro

6 MEVAGISSEY

In days gone by, this beguiling little port relied on the pilchard fishing industry for its living. Although the shoals of pilchards have now gone, Mevagissey is still a thriving fishing port. It remains a timeless, unspoilt place of great charm, with rows of colour-washed cottages tumbling down the cliff-side in tiers, with many nooks and crannies to explore.

P WC & 🚂 - St. Austell

7 LOST GARDENS OF HELIGAN

On the outskirts of Mevagissey are the romantically named 'Lost Gardens of Heligan', the largest garden reclamation project in Britain. Here you will find four-walled gardens, together with extensive rockeries, shrubberies and a fascinating area known as the Jungle

(a kind of rocky ravine featuring palms, tree ferns and plants from Australia) all being restored to their Victorian magnificence. The original gardens were created in about 1780, around the Tremayne family house. They fell into neglect and remained untouched for over 70 years, when they were rescued by Tim Smit and his associates. The restoration project began in 1990.

Open daily all year, except Christmas Day.
📞 01726 845100

P WC 🍴 & 🚂 - St. Austell

8 POLPERRO

One of the showplaces of Cornwall, Polperro probably typifies the image that most people have of the West Country - a quaint village of granite and colour-washed cottages clustering round a small harbour. During the summer season

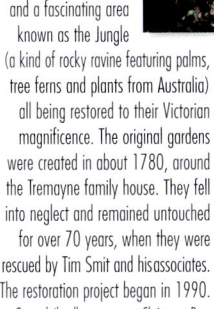

cars are banned from the village. There are regular horse and cart rides from the large car park on the outskirts down to the centre. To escape the crowds, climb the steps between houses on the right of the quay, giving access to the cliff path.

P WC 🍴 & 🚂 - Looe

DRYSTONE WALLS

Amongst the most typical landscape features of Cornwall are the drystone walls, more commonly used than hedges as stock barriers between fields. Typically, a drystone wall is constructed by building two outer walls of large stones, tapering inwards, with an infill of smaller stones, held together without the use of mortar. In Cornwall, a regional variation developed. Instead of a rock infill between the outer walls, soil was used, which was then planted with typical hedgerow plants, growing on the top of the wall.

Hidden Delights

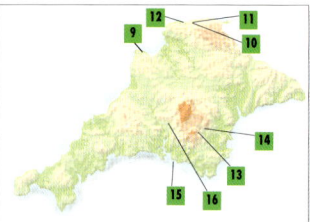

9 CLOVELLY

Clovelly is a fascinating place to explore, and if you can arrange to visit out of season, you will find it remarkably unspoilt when the crowds have gone. The main street leading down to the tiny harbour is exceptionally steep and breathtakingly beautiful. Surprisingly, cars have been banned for many years, but not because of its recent popularity. A Victorian lady-of-the-manor, Mrs. Christine Hamlyn, had the foresight to protect the village from cars and over-development.

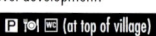

11 LYNMOUTH

At the foot of the cliffs lies Lynmouth, a small settlement with a lovely harbour.

It is linked to Lynton, its sister village, by a very steep road and by a cliff railway. Operated by carefully controlled water tanks and with a gradient of 1 in 1.75, the railway provides a most exhilarating ride. Again, most visitors tend to stay in the village centre, but just a short walk away lies some of Devon's finest scenic delights.

📞 01598 753486

10 LYNTON

Lynmouth and Lynton are twin settlements on the spectacular north Devon coast. They have some of England's highest cliffs (900 ft/274 m) to the coastward side, and arguably the most dramatic scenery of the West Country inland. Lynton is located at the top of the cliffs and has developed into a settlement of some size. Located within the Exmoor National Park the surrounding hills provide many woodland walks.

12 VALLEY OF THE ROCKS

The Valley of the Rocks lies just west of Lynton and is best reached along the cliff path. It offers some of the most dramatic scenes in Devon. Nature has fashioned the rocks into spectacular shapes, towering above the valley floor by as much as 800 ft (240 m). Of particular note are the Castle Rock (the tallest of the rocks here), Devil's Cheesewring and the White Lady. In the quieter corners, the more observant may be lucky enough to catch sight of one of the wild goats that live in the valley.

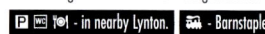

DEVON

DARTMOOR

The wild expanse of Dartmoor holds many surprises; indeed, the list of hidden places to explore in solitude is almost too numerous to mention, despite the huge popularity of the National Park. Fortunately, few areas on the moor suffer from too many visitors, and the following places are a delight to visit at any time of the year. Both are located in the northeast corner of Dartmoor.

13 BECKY FALLS

From the village of Manaton a small signed road leads through thick woodland to Becky Falls, an excellent spot for a picnic. The waters here tumble over the rocks in a cascade over 70 ft (21 m) high.

P - Newton Abbot

14 LUSTLEIGH

Lustleigh village is very picturesque and contains some fine granite buildings. The 15th-century church has a screen featuring the pomegranate badge of Catherine of Aragon. Nearby is a beautiful wooded gorge, known as Lustleigh Cleave, ideal country for walking.

P - Newton Abbot

15 NOSS MAYO

Noss Mayo is a picturesque and unspoilt little fishing village on the South Devon coast between Salcombe and Plymouth. It stands in a sheltered position on the banks of Newton Creek, a small tributary of the River Yealm. Surprisingly remote, its safe harbour is still used by fishermen and was once popular as a smugglers' haunt.

P WC I&O - Plymouth

16 LYDFORD GORGE

There is much to see at Lydford, on the western fringes of Dartmoor. In the 9th century, Lydford was an important fortified town, but is now no more than a village. The 12th-century ruined castle (English Heritage) was once used as a courthouse and prison. Nearby, Lydford Gorge (National Trust) is a spectacular natural ravine, with many delightful waterfalls and rock pools. The largest of these, the White Lady Waterfall, can be seen at the head of the gorge, which is where most of the crowds congregate, but just a short distance away lies peace and solitude.

Castle open at various times. Gorge open Mar.-Oct. daily; Nov-Mar., waterfall entrance only. 01822 820320

P WC I&O - Okehampton

LAND OF LEGEND

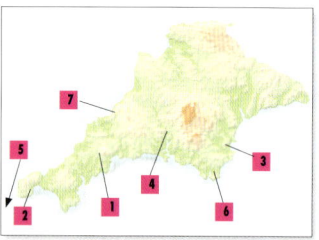

No area of Britain is more steeped in history and legend than the West Country, perhaps inspired by the dramatic coastal and moorland scenery. Stories abound of legendary giants, heroes such as King Arthur, lost kingdoms and tales of shipwrecks and piracy. Many sites associated with this rich tapestry of story-telling can be visited, offering further fuel to the imagination.

1 THE HERMIT OF ROCHE

Near the village of Roche in Cornwall is this rocky outcrop, crowned by a ruined chapel and hermitage. It was once the home of St. Gonand, a leper. The chapel is said to have been visited by Tregeagle, a spirit haunted by demons, who was sent on his way by the hermit who lived there. The chapel can be freely visited at any time.

P at Roche   **🚂** - Roche

2 MYSTERIOUS STONES

Both Devon and Cornwall are littered with prehistoric standing stones. Many of these monuments are of unknown purpose and have attracted various stories. The Men-an-tol stone, near Penzance (on the Madron to Morrah road), in Cornwall, was believed to cure rickets in children if they were passed through the hole. Lanyon Quoit (shown right) was probably the central chamber of a Stone-Age tomb.

P   **🚂** - Penzance

3 HAUNTINGS

Ghost stories abound in this region. One of the most haunted sites is the remote Berry Pomeroy Castle (English Heritage), near Totnes in Devon. Two sisters of the Pomeroy family, former owners of the castle in medieval times, fell in love with the same man. Eleanor, lady of the castle, was so jealous of her beautiful sister, Margaret, that she had her imprisoned in a tower, where she died. Margaret reputedly still haunts the castle, but to see her means certain death!

Berry Pomeroy Castle, near Totnes: open daily, Apr.-Nov.

📞 01803 866618

P **WC** **🍴** **♿**   **🚂** - Totnes

CORNWALL & DEVON

4 EL DRAQUE

Sir Francis Drake (known to his Spanish enemies as 'El Draque' - the dragon) assumed legendary status following his circumnavigation of the world in 1577-80 and his part in defeating the Spanish Armada in 1588. He was born near Tavistock in Devon, where a statue of him can be seen. Other places associated with Drake are Plymouth and Buckland Abbey (see page 27), where he lived in semi-retirement, which is now a museum to the great man. Buckland Abbey (National Trust), Yelverton, Devon: Open Fri.-Wed., Apr.-Oct.; weekends only in winter.

📞 01822 853607   P WC 🍴 ♿   🚂 - Calstock

5 ISLES OF SCILLY

Claimed to be the last remnants of the lost kingdom of Lyonesse, the Isles of Scilly are the southernmost islands of Britain. Of over 100 islands and rocks, only five are inhabited. The islands have a timeless charm and enjoy the mildest climate in Britain: many subtropical plants flourish there. Apart from tourism, the main industry is flower-growing. Like jewels set in an azure sea, the islands can be reached by boat from Penzance or helicopter. For details of flights, contact The Heliport, Penzance

📞 01736 363871   P WC 🍴 ♿   🚂 - Penzance

6 SHIPWRECKS

The West Country is famous for its stories of 'wreckers', people who lured ships onto the rocks with lanterns to mimic lighthouses and then stole away with their cargoes when ships foundered. The heavy seas still claim many ships, such as the Demetrios, whose wreck can still be seen off Prawle Point in Devon.

P WC 🍴 ♿   🚂 - Totnes

7 KING ARTHUR

Many legends of the West Country are associated with King Arthur. Traditionally, Tintagel in Cornwall is reputed to be King Arthur's birthplace (see page 25); a cave, on the beach below the castle, is still known as Merlin's Cave. There are the remains of a medieval castle and 5th-century monastery (English Heritage) at Tintagel, dramatically sited on the cliff-tops. Recent archaeological discoveries in the vicinity of Tintagel have now established a tangible link with Arthur. Tintagel Castle, Tintagel Head: open daily all year, except 24-26 Dec. and 1 Jan.   📞 01840 770328

P WC 🍴   🚂 - Bodmin

HISTORICAL HERITAGE

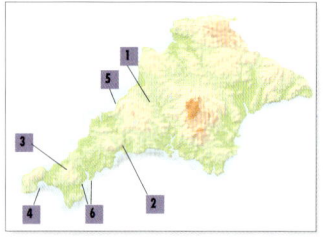

The heritage of Cornwall is unique in England. There are fewer grand houses, castles and soaring monastic ruins than in most other counties, but each has its own very distinctive Cornish character. Many of the historic sites of Cornwall are located amidst spectacular cliff scenery, adding immeasurably to their atmospheric charm.

1 LAUNCESTON CASTLE

Launceston town centre

Pronounced 'Lawnson' by the locals, this used to be the capital of Cornwall, until it relinquished the title to Bodmin in 1838. The town is dominated by its magnificent Norman castle (English Heritage). Its somewhat cramped centre contains the remains of a shell keep, built around an unusual circular tower keep, with fine views over the town and countryside beyond. The town stands proudly on a hill near the Devon border and contains many fascinating and quaint old corners, as well as being a busy modern shopping centre. Nearby are the Launceston Steam Railway and Tamar Otter Park. The castle is open daily, except 24-26 Dec and 1 Jan 📞 01566 772365 P WC ⑩ ♿ in Launceston   🚂 - Liskeard

2 RESTORMEL CASTLE

Off the A390 at Lostwithiel

On the outskirts of Lostwithiel can be found the impressive ruins of Restormel Castle (English Heritage). What remains is the shell keep (one of the finest in the country) of a medieval castle, first built by the Normans. The floors and roofs have long-since disappeared, but the walls and battlement walk are very well preserved. The castle stands in beautiful, wooded grounds, bedecked with exotic rhododendron flowers in early summer. Lostwithiel itself is a small, attractive market town, with many interesting craft and antique shops. Open daily, Apr.-Nov. 📞 01208 872687 P WC ⑩ ♿   🚂 - Lostwithiel

3 TRERICE HOUSE

Kestle Hill, Near Newquay

A delightful small, secluded Elizabethan manor house, built in 1571 and now administered by the National Trust. The house has an early gabled facade and contains fine fireplaces and ceilings, with a wonderful collection of clocks and furniture. There is an unusual museum of lawnmowers and a small garden. Open at various times, Apr-Oct. 📞 01637 875404 P WC ⑩ ♿   🚂 - Newquay

CORNWALL

4 ST. MICHAEL'S MOUNT

Mount's Bay, Marazion

The magnificent jewel of St. Michael's Mount rises from the deep blue waters of Mount's Bay like a fairytale castle. This small rocky island lies just half a mile offshore from Marazion and can be reached by a stone causeway at low tide, or by boat at high tide. The island houses a small village and harbour and takes its name from a similar

island (Mont St. Michel) off the Normandy coast. The Greeks knew the place as Ictis, when the Cornish traded tin with them. At various times in its history it has been home to a church, a monastery, a castle and a mansion, all now incorporated into the present house, which is owned by the National Trust. Open Apr.-Oct. weekdays. 📞 01736 710507

🅿 on mainland at Marazion

🚻 🍴 🚌 - Penzance

5 TINTAGEL

Tintagel Head

Tintagel Castle (English Heritage), on Cornwall's dramatic north coast, has long been associated with the legends of King Arthur (see page 23). Like St. Michael's Mount, the castle stands on a site formerly occupied by a monastery, in this case of 5th-century Celtic foundation. The monastery was later converted into a fortified camp and in 1145, a castle was built there. Only scant remains can be seen today, but the setting is truly spectacular. Tintagel is popular with tourists in high summer, so try to visit out of season if you want to appreciate the quiet charm of the neighbouring village, famed for the Old Post Office, a 14th-century manor house (shown above). Castle: open daily all year, except 24-26 Dec. and 1 Jan. Not suitable for wheelchair users. A Landrover service operates in summer, for which there is a small charge.

📞 01840 770328

🅿 🚻 🍴 in Tintagel village - castle half-a-mile walk. 🚌 - Bodmin

6 ST. MAWES & PENDENNIS CASTLES

St. Mawes Castle: on the A3078; Pendennis Castle: Pendennis Head, Falmouth

The twin castles of St. Mawes and Pendennis (English Heritage) stand at either side of Carrick Roads, a wide, deep-water inlet that forms the estuary of seven Cornish rivers. The castles protected Falmouth harbour and in particular the Tudor dockyard established there by Henry VIII. After Henry broke from the Church of Rome he feared an invasion by the Catholic countries of Spain and France and protected the south coast of Britain with a chain of defensive fortifications. St. Mawes (shown above) and Pendennis Castles were begun in 1542 and remain perfectly preserved today. Both have massive semi-circular and angular bastions to carry heavy artillery. If you intend visiting both, why not catch the ferry across the beautiful Fal estuary: a magical experience.

English Heritage. Open daily all year, except 24-26 Dec. and 1 Jan. 📞 01326 316594.
For ferry details (foot passengers) 📞 01326 313201; for cars 📞 01872 72463

🅿 🚻 🍴 ♿ 🚌 - Truro/Falmouth

THE LANGUAGE OF CORNWALL

Cornwall was relatively unaffected by the Roman conquest of Britain and so retained many of its ancient Celtic customs. For many years it was a small, independent country with its own kings. Even today, it claims stronger cultural links with other Celtic countries, such as Wales and Brittany in France, than with the rest of England. Cornwall also had its own language, recognised as being independent of other Celtic tongues, still evident in the unusual place names. Few people speak the language today.

HISTORICAL HERITAGE

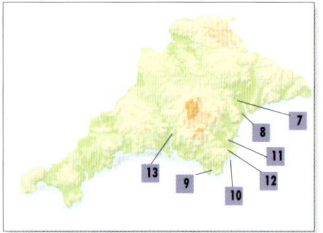

Devon seems to specialise in presenting the unsuspecting traveller with sights of sheer delight. The scenery of Devon is more varied than that of neighbouring Cornwall; so too is the range of its architectural heritage, from mighty Norman castles and elegant stately homes to monastic ruins and a magnificent medieval cathedral.

7 EXETER CATHEDRAL

Palace Gate, Exeter, Devon

Exeter possesses the only medieval cathedral in the West Country (Cornwall did not acquire its cathedral at Truro until 1880). The first cathedral to stand on this site was in Saxon times, but this was replaced between 1107-37 by a Norman structure. The nave and the impressive west front were rebuilt during the 14th century, and decorated with rows of statues. Unusually, there is no central tower, which makes the nave particularly impressive as it is seen uninterrupted from end to end. Despite its great bulk, the cathedral is well screened from view by tall shops and houses, giving it an added charm. Open daily, all year.

P WC ⚑ nearby in town. ♿ 🚐 - Exeter

8 POWDERHAM CASTLE

Off the A379, south of Powderham village, Devon

Powderham Castle is another of Devon's wonderful surprises. Much of the present building dates from the period 1760-1860 and is sumptuously decorated in Georgian and Victorian styles. Of special interest are the painted stairwell and the Marble Hall. But all is not what it seems, for the house is much older than it looks and at its core are the remains of a 14th-century castle. This was the seat of the Courtenay family and is still the family home of the Earls of Devon. The castle, built in soft, pink-tinged stone, is surrounded by a deer park. Open Sun.-Fri., Apr-Oct. ☎ 01626 890243

P WC ⚑ ♿ 🚐 - Starcross

9 YARDE FARMHOUSE

Malborough, Kingsbridge, Devon

A rare opportunity to visit an historic Devon farmhouse, still lived in by the family who own it and run the property as a working farm. The entire complex is currently undergoing extensive restoration, to recreate an authentic 16th/17th-century farm. On display are various historic cooking utensils and cider-making equipment. Outside are an ancient apple orchard, cottage-style gardens, a meadow walk, farm animals and a pets corner.

Open Sun., Easter-Sept. ☎ 01548 842367

P WC ⚑ ♿ 🚐 - Totnes

DEVON

10 DARTMOUTH CASTLE

Off the B3205, southeast of Dartmouth, Devon (reached by ferry)

Dartmouth Castle (English Heritage) lies in a truly stunning setting, situated on a rocky promontory at the edge of the Dart estuary. The castle was built in the 1480s and

is believed to be the earliest coastal defence work specifically designed for use by artillery. The castle saw action during the Civil War, when it was taken first by the Royalists and then by Parliament, under General Fairfax. His army retook the castle after a siege lasting just a few hours. Open daily all year, except 24-26 Dec. and 1 Jan. 📞 01803 833588

[P] [WC] [🍴] [♿] 🚌 - Kingswear

11 COMPTON CASTLE

Off the A3022, west of Torquay, Devon

More a fortified manor house than a castle proper, Compton Castle's stark granite walls could nevertheless

withstand a determined attack. Inside, the great hall and other rooms have been beautifully restored. It was once the home of the Elizabethan explorer Sir Humphrey Gilbert, one of the early colonisers of North America. Open Apr.-Oct. 📞 01803 872112

[P] [WC] [🍴] [♿] 🚌 - Torquay

12 TOTNES CASTLE

The Butterwalk, Totnes, Devon

The charming old town of Totnes (see page 34) is a must for any visitor to Devon, dominated by the ruins of its castle (English Heritage) on the hill overlooking the town centre. First built in the 11th century as a simple Norman motte and bailey, the original timber defences were replaced in stone in the 13th century. It still preserves a fine shell keep (a circular wall surmounting the top of the mound) from which fine views of the surrounding countryside can be had. Open daily, Apr.-Oct; Wed.-Sun., Nov-Mar; closed 24-26 Dec and 1 Jan.
📞 01803 864406

[P] [WC] [🍴] - in town. 🚌 - Totnes

13 BUCKLAND ABBEY

Yelverton, Devon

Buckland Abbey, a few miles north of Plymouth, has had an interesting, if somewhat chequered history. The original abbey dates from about 1278 and flourished throughout the Middle Ages. It was suppressed by Henry VIII at the Dissolution and purchased, in 1541, by Sir Richard Grenville, an Elizabethan sea captain. The abbey ruins were converted into a magnificent house.
The next owner was Sir Francis Drake, Grenville's arch rival, who purchased the house through intermediaries to keep his identity secret. The abbey remained in the Drake family until this century. Managed jointly by the National Trust and Plymouth City Council, the abbey contains many fascinating maritime relics and Drake memorabilia. Open Fri.-Wed., Apr.-Oct. and at weekends only in winter.
📞 01822 853607

[P] [WC] [🍴] [♿]

🚌 - Bere Alston

CIDER

Cider was probably the first alcoholic drink brewed by man and has been brewed in Britain since at least Celtic (pre-Roman) times. Today, Britain is the world's biggest cider producer, with over 75% of all apples grown here used to make cider.
In the 14th century, children were sometimes baptised with cider and up until the 19th century some farm labourers received part of their wages in the form of cider. Stronger than most beers, there is a prominent cider-making tradition in the West Country. Why not try one of the many local brews (known as 'scrumpy') while you are here!

BEAUTIFUL GARDENS

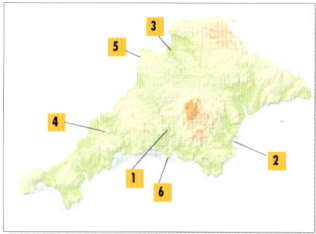

The gardens of Devon and Cornwall, particularly those on the more sheltered south coasts, are unique in Britain. They benefit from the effects of the Gulf Stream which brings milder air than is generally experienced by the rest of the country, even in winter, allowing lush, semi-tropical plants to flourish outdoors.

1 COTEHELE HOUSE & GARDENS
Near Calstock, Cornwall

On the west bank of the River Tamar, near Calstock, can be found the house and gardens of Cotehele (National Trust). There are several gardens here built on different levels and surrounding a medieval house (late 15th-century) of grey granite. Inside, there are many fine tapestries and original furnishings, while outside are ponds and banks of rhododendrons. Beside the river can also be seen a restored boathouse and water mill.

House open Apr.-Oct. Gardens open all year. 📞 01579 351346   P WC 🍴 ♿   🚆 - Calstock

2 TORRE ABBEY GARDENS
The Kings Drive, Torquay, Devon

Torre Abbey was originally founded in 1196. After the Dissolution it was acquired by the Cary family, who converted some of the buildings into a fine mansion. The monastic remains are the most extensive in Devon and Cornwall. Now owned by Torbay Borough Council, the abbey was purchased in 1930 to house their growing art collection. The house is surrounded by beautiful gardens, famed for their semi-tropical plants, which flourish in the mild Devon air. The gardens are mostly formal, skilfully using the abbey ruins as a backdrop. Open daily, Easter-Nov. 📞 01803 293593

P WC 🍴 (nearby in Torquay town) ♿

🚆 - Torquay

3 TAPLEY PARK GARDENS
On the B3233, Instow, Devon

These beautiful gardens have been owned by the same family for almost 300 years, with each successive generation adding its own touch. There is a lake, at the bottom of a ravine, a woodland walk, walled kitchen garden and a recently restored Italian garden. There is also a plant sales area and children's woodland play area. The house and garden look out over the bay to Lundy Island. Tours of the house can be arranged by appointment. Open Sun.-Fri., Easter-Oct.

📞 01271 860897

P WC 🍴 ♿   🚆 - Barnstaple

DEVON & CORNWALL

4 PENCARROW HOUSE & GARDENS

Washaway, Bodmin, Cornwall

Pencarrow House, near Bodmin, is approached by a mile-long drive through an ancient British encampment, flanked by huge rhododendrons, blue hydrangeas and specimen conifers. The fine Georgian country house was completed c.1770 by Sir John Molesworth, whose descendants still live there today. The house contains a superb collection of paintings, furniture and porcelain. The Grade II-listed gardens are wonderful and include a lake, woodland and Italian gardens, a rockery and an ice-house.

Open Sun.-Thur. Easter-Oct. 01208 841369   P WC ᵀᴼᴸ ♿ 🚂 - Bodmin Parkway

See also The Lost Gardens of Heligan, page 19

5 HARTLAND ABBEY GARDENS

Off the A39 between Hartland and Hartland Quay, Devon

Originally an Augustinian monastery built in 1157, Hartland Abbey was the last monastery to be dissolved by Henry VIII. He gave it to the keeper of his wine cellar, William Abbott, who won it in a game of tennis! The abbey buildings were converted into a very comfortable house, still owned by William Abbott's descendants. Situated in a beautiful valley, the house contains fine furniture and paintings and sits amidst glorious gardens, partly laid out by Gertrude Jekyll, with 18th-century walled gardens, and herbaceous, tender and rare plants. There is also a small museum and woodland walk leading to a delightful cove.

Open Mon., Wed., Thur. and Sun., May-Sept.; also Tues., Jul.-Aug. only.   01237 441264

P WC ᵀᴼᴸ ♿ 🚂 - Barnstaple

6 MOUNT EDGCUMBE

Near Cremyll, Torpoint, Cornwall (reached by ferry from Plymouth or road via Tamar Bridge through Cornwall)

In 1553, the Edgcumbe family moved here from their house at Cotehele, 10 miles (16 km) to the north. They built a magnificent house and surrounded it with fine gardens. The gardens are now a country park covering some 900 acres. They contain many rare plants and also the National Camellia Collection. It is said that Medina Sedonia, commander of the Spanish Armada, vowed to live at Edgcumbe if the Spanish were successful in defeating the English.

Gardens open daily all year.

 01752 822236

P WC ᵀᴼᴸ ♿ 🚂 - Plymouth

MUSEUMS AND GALLERIES

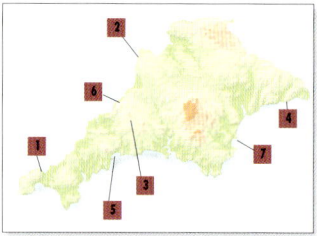

The West Country is rich in museums of every type and probably supports the largest colony of artists in Britain outside London. Artists first became attracted to the area in the 19th century, drawn here by the mild climate and clear light. Artists from both Britain and abroad are still attracted to the area, congregating mostly around the fishing villages of St.Ives and Newlyn on the Penwith Peninsula.

1 TATE GALLERY,
Porthmeor Beach, St. Ives, Cornwall

Dramatically sited overlooking the sea at Porthmeor Beach, St. Ives, the Tate Gallery was opened in 1993 and presents changing displays of 20th-century art in the context of Cornwall, focusing on the modern tradition. Displays are drawn from the Tate Gallery Collection of British and Modern Art, who manage the purpose-built gallery on behalf of Cornwall County Council. The gallery also has an education studio and holds exhibitions. There is a charming roof-top café.
Open daily, all year. 01736 796226 nearby, - St. Ives

---

2 HARTLAND QUAY MUSEUM
Harbour Road, Stoke, Devon

Hartland Quay Museum is devoted to the history, rural industries and natural features (including flora and fauna) of the spectacular stretch of coastline at Hartland. The exhibits illustrate 400 years of local shipwrecks, smuggling and life-saving at Hartland Quay. There are no facilities at the museum, but some are available at the Hartland Quay Hotel which is immediately opposite. Open Easter week, then Whitsun-Sept.
01288 331353
 - Barnstaple

3 JAMAICA INN MUSEUMS
Off the A30 at Bolventor, Cornwall

The author Daphne du Maurier stayed at the Jamaica Inn in 1930, and it became her inspiration for the book of the same name. In addition to full pub and restaurant facilities, the inn also offers accommodation (though beware, the place is haunted!), a gift shop and several museums, including a museum of smuggling (using tableaux, light and sound), Mr. Potter's Museum of Curiosity, an exhibition devoted to du Maurier and a children's play area. Open daily throughout the year.
01566 86250
 - Bodmin Parkway

DEVON & CORNWALL

4 TRAMWAY MUSEUM

Harbour Road, Seaton, Devon

Explore the beautiful Axe Valley by tram! The Tramway Museum at Seaton is unique in that it operates working trams purpose-built to traditional designs, but at about half the original size. The trams run on a narrow-gauge track a distance of 3 miles (5 km) between Seaton and Colyton, alongside the beautiful River Axe. They depart every 20 minutes - and tram driving lessons are available for the more adventurous.

Open daily, Easter-Oct., then weekends until Christmas

📞 01297 720375   P WC 🍴 ♿   🚂 - Axminster

5 CHARLESTOWN SHIPWRECK & HERITAGE CENTRE

Quay Road, Charlestown, Cornwall

The excellent Shipwreck and Heritage Centre contains one of the largest collections of maritime memorabilia and artefacts in the country. There are also various special exhibitions, which are regularly changed, and replica historic ships tie up in the harbour on occasion. Open daily, Mar.-Oct; by appointment at other times.

📞 01726 69897

P WC 🍴 ♿
🚂 - St Austell

6 BOSCASTLE MUSEUM OF WITCHCRAFT

Boscastle, Cornwall

One of the most unusual and interesting museums in the West Country, the Witchcraft Musem is located at the historic and unspoilt port of Boscastle. Inside are many items associated with witchcraft and the 'old ways', but this is no mere gimmick of the tourist industry; it is a genuine attempt to explain pre-Christian beliefs and the persecution of so-called 'witches' in later centuries. The church in Boscastle was restored by the novelist Thomas Hardy, who married the rector's sister-in-law, Emma.

Open Easter-Oct.   📞 01840 250111

P WC 🍴 - Boscastle.   🚂 - Bodmin

STARGAZY PIE

This Cornish recipe was once peculiar to the pretty village of Mousehole (pronounced 'Mowzell'), near Penzance, but it is now served elsewhere too. According to local tradition, a fisherman by the name of Tom Bawcock saved the village from starvation by putting out to sea in a storm one winter's night. He returned with a huge catch, and to commemorate the event a special pie was made using whole fish, with their heads poking out through the pastry rim, known locally as 'Stargazy Pie'.

7 TORQUAY MUSEUM

Babbacombe Road, Torquay, Devon

The borough of Torbay has two fine museums at Brixham and Torquay, both very different in character. Torquay Museum is the oldest museum in Devon, with eight galleries, ranging in interest from archaeology and natural history to Victorian history. There is also an Agatha Christie exhibition and a display of finds from Kent's Cavern (see page 12). Open Mon.-Fri. all year; also weekends Easter-Oct.   📞 01803 293975

P opposite WC 🍴   🚂 - Torquay

ABOUT TOWN

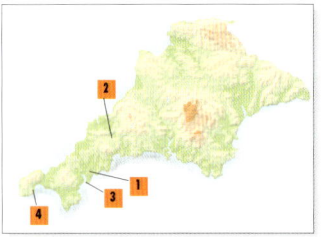

The towns of Cornwall are not particularly remarkable from an architectural point of view, though that is not to say they are without interest. Although there are no great centres or impressive municipal buildings, visitors who are content to explore on foot the many quaint villages scattered around the coastline will be rewarded with discoveries of the hidden treasures they contain.

1 TRURO

Since 1989, Truro has been the administrative centre of Cornwall. The town is dominated by its cathedral (the only one in Cornwall) which was built only between 1880-1920 to reflect Truro's growing importance. It was the first Anglican cathedral to be built in England since St. Paul's in London in 1675. Modern Truro is a mixture of the old and the new. Few traces of its medieval past remain (both its castle and Dominican friary have disappeared) and there are large areas of modern development, not all of it good. There are some fine Georgian terraces, however, and overall it is a very pleasant town with well laid out streets and good shopping; probably the best in the county. Its central location makes it an ideal base from which to explore the other delights of Cornwall.

🚆 - Truro

2 BODMIN

Between 1835-1989, Bodmin was the county town of Cornwall. During the Victorian period, the town prospered and many buildings were erected in the town centre, including barracks and a prison, both now fitted out as museums. The town is far older, however, and dates from the 6th century, when St. Petroc is supposed to have settled there. The main A30 trunk road used to run right through the heart of the town, causing huge traffic delays. Happily, the town is now bypassed and has reverted to being an attractive market town. It is a lively, bustling place with good shopping and makes an ideal base from which to explore the wilds of Bodmin Moor.

🚆 - Bodmin Parkway

CORNWALL

3 FALMOUTH

Falmouth occupies a unique setting at the mouth of one of the finest natural harbours in Britain. It quickly developed from a small fishing village into an important port that grew to become the second busiest in England, after London. It declined as sailing ships gave way to steam, but enjoyed renewed prosperity after the arrival of the railway in 1863. The old town occupies a small peninsula, with new developments spreading out behind. Its sheltered location has ensured its popularity in recent times as a yachting centre and holiday destination. The old town is quite delightful, its bustling main street decked with flowers in the summer, with several narrow alleyways and streets leading down to the water's edge.

- Falmouth

4 PENZANCE

One of the most evocatively named towns in Cornwall (due in no small part to the Gilbert and Sullivan operetta *Pirates of Penzance*), Penzance is now one of the county's liveliest holiday towns. It is also the gateway to the Isles of Scilly, with ferries and helicopters offering regular services to these delightful islands. Penzance enjoys a mild climate on the west end of Mount's Bay, and semi-tropical plants flourish in the area. It became a fashionable watering-hole for London society after the arrival of the railway in 1857, and soon sported many fine hotels. Modern Penzance offers holidaymakers everything they could want, from good shopping, museums, gardens and pubs to an excellent choice of hotels and restaurants.

- Penzance

CREAM TEAS

No visit to the West Country would be complete without a delicious cream tea. The usual ingredients are a pot of tea, two scones, jam and plentiful supplies of clotted cream. Cornish cream has a butterfat content of about 60%, which is slightly less than Devon cream. Several places will arrange for a delivery of fresh cream to coincide with your arrival home; ask for details where you see the sign.

About Town

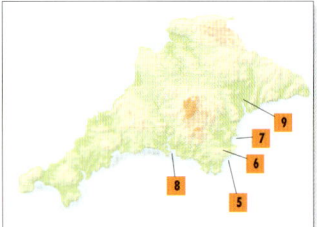

By contrast to neighbouring Cornwall, Devon boasts several large metropolises, impressive by any standards. Plymouth has long naval associations and has become a mecca for those seeking nightlife. The county has several other important towns, as well as small market towns and bustling centres of commerce, all with a distinctive historical flavour and individual character.

5 DARTMOUTH

Dartmouth is an ancient port and attractive town standing near the estuary of the River Dart, one of the most beautiful rivers in Britain. It has long had associations with the Navy and is home to the Royal Naval Training College. The town enjoys a beautiful setting, both beside the river and straddling a steep hill inland. Today it is also popular as a yachting centre on the wide estuary. The old town was protected by a small castle in the late 15th century which was attacked by Sir Thomas Fairfax in the Civil War. Dartmouth is dominated by the river and there are regular ferry crossings to the opposite bank. The steep, narrow streets of the old town are fascinating to explore, containing a charming mixture of building styles.

🚆 - Kingswear   then ferry to Dartmouth

6 TOTNES

The River Dart is navigable up to and beyond Totnes. Totnes is another delightful old town that has managed to preserve the best of its past, albeit still embracing the needs of modern living. Sited on a steep hill, its narrow streets and alleyways climb from the quayside to the ancient walled town.
Traces of the medieval town walls still survive, as does the castle, an excellent example of a Norman motte and bailey. There is much to see and do here, including the Guildhall and Totnes Museum. There are also frequent river trips to Dartmouth, and plenty of fine shops, facilities and restaurants. The town is ideally placed for touring the Dartmoor National Park.

🚆 - Totnes

DEVON

7 TORQUAY

Torquay is built on a range of hills overlooking the sea. Many of the buildings are painted white, giving the place a real Mediterranean feel, an atmosphere further enhanced by the exceptionally mild climate that allows sub-tropical plants to flourish. The town is very elegant and boasts a full range of visitor facilities, including excellent hotels and restaurants, theatres, nightclubs, entertainment

centres and several fine beaches. Fortunately, it still manages to avoid being over-commercialized. The town became a fashionable watering place during the Napoleonic wars, when it was just a small fishing community known as Torre Quay. Together with the neighbouring towns of Paignton and Brixham, it now forms part of the Torbay holiday coast.

🚂 - Torquay

8 PLYMOUTH

The largest town in Devon, and the Southwest, Plymouth is also the most cosmopolitan. Following devastating bombing raids during World War II, the centre was extensively rebuilt along imaginative lines, with wide streets and tree-lined boulevards. It is a vibrant city, with something for everyone, boasting several cinemas, theatres, a casino and a nightlife that is second to none in the West Country. There are several traffic-free shopping centres and a host of other attractions and restaurants catering for all tastes. The old town down by the quay-side still survives and the wide, open expanse of the Hoe, with its statue of Sir Francis Drake, makes this a truly magnificent resort. Regular ferry services operate from the docks to Santander in northern Spain, and Roscoff in France.

🚂 - Plymouth

9 EXETER

Although not the largest town in Devon, Exeter has always been the county town and administrative centre of the region. It is a major focus of air, rail and road networks in the Southwest and is the terminus for the M5, the only stretch of motorway in the region. The city centre was severely damaged by bombs during World War II, but miraculously, many old buildings survive. One of the most fascinating survivors is the unique system of underground tunnels (part of the medieval water and drainage system). Regular tours are conducted throughout the year from outside Boots Arcade in the High Street (call 01392 265858 for details). Exeter Cathedral is another survivor and is truly magnificent. Modern Exeter has been tastefully rebuilt and prides itself on being the principal shopping and commercial centre of the area.

🚂 - Exeter

CLOTTED CREAM

The traditional method of making clotted cream for cream teas is to take a quantity of milk (preferably from the evening milking, which is creamier) and pour it into a flat dish to settle overnight. The following morning, the dish of milk is placed inside a larger pan, filled with water, and placed on a stove to heat the water, but not boil the cream (a process known as scalding). After about half an hour, the pan containing the cream is removed and allowed to stand overnight. The following morning the cream is skimmed off and ready to eat!

DIARY OF EVENTS AND FESTIVALS

On these two pages are listed various events and festivals that are held on a regular basis in Devon and Cornwall throughout the year. They are listed by month and contain brief details of the events. Although most are held annually, the exact dates vary from year to year so as to fall on convenient weekends or public holidays. You are advised to contact the nearest Tourist Information Centre (addresses and telephone numbers are listed on pages 42-44 of this guide) for further information regarding dates, times and prices of admission to avoid possible disappointment, or for details of any one-off events.

JANUARY

STEAM UP
Coldharbour Mill (Working Wool Museum), Uffculme, Cullompton, Devon. *Steam engines and machinery for spinning and weaving.*
☎ 01884 840960

FEBRUARY

AVOCET CRUISES
Exmouth Docks, Devon. *Winter river cruises for bird-watching enthusiasts (various dates).*
☎ 01392 53215

ST. IVES FEAST CELEBRATIONS
St. Ives, Cornwall. *Mayoral Procession and hurling of Silver Ball from church tower; various other events.*
☎ 01736 797840

APRIL

FLAMBARDS TRADITIONAL EASTER BONNET PARADE AND COMPETITION
Helston, Cornwall. *Theme park, Easter Bonnet Parade, competitions.*
☎ 01326 573404.

BICTON HORSE TRIALS
East Budleigh, Devon. *Various horse-riding and jumping events.*
☎ 01404 87296

CAMBORNE TREVITHICK DAY
Camborne, Cornwall. *Steam engines, vintage vehicles, organs, birds and street theatre to celebrate Richard Trevithick.*
☎ 01209 712941

MAY

WORLD PILOT GIG CHAMPIONSHIPS
Isles of Scilly. *Rowing championships in the open sea.*
☎ 01720 422536

UFFCULME SHEEP SHOW
Coldharbour Mill (Working Wool Museum), Uffculme, Cullompton, Devon. *Rare sheep breeds, spinning and other country crafts, steam engines.*
☎ 01884 840960

HELSTON FURRY DANCE
Helston, Cornwall. *Spring Festival, with various processional dances through the town and street floral decorations.*
☎ 01326 565431

WISCOMBE PARK SPEED HILL CLIMB
Southleigh, Colyton, Devon. *Speed hill climb for vintage cars.*
📞 01734 302439

JUNE
ROYAL CORNWALL SHOW
Wadebridge, Cornwall. *Countryside show, livestock, flower show, craft and trade stalls.*
📞 01208 812183

BRIXHAM INTERNATIONAL TRAWLER RACE & QUAY FESTIVAL
Brixham, Devon. *Trawler racing, water events, stalls.*
📞 01803 846182

POWDERHAM HORSE TRIALS
Powderham Castle, Kenton, Devon. *Show-jumping, dressage and cross-country events.*
📞 01626 890243

JULY
PLYMOUTH INTERNATIONAL BOAT ANGLING FESTIVAL
Sutton Harbour, Plymouth. *Competition sea angling.*
📞 01822 854761

ST. PETER'S FAIR WEEK
Holsworthy, Devon. *Traditional local fair, furry dance, street entertainment and ale-tasting.*
📞 01409 253441

TREGONY CARNIVAL
Tregony, Truro, Cornwall. *Traditional street carnival.*
📞 01872 530357

AIR SHOW
Royal Navy Air Station, Culdrose, Helston, Cornwall. *Military and civilian air show.*
📞 01326 552461

AUGUST
INTERNATIONAL AIR SHOW, RAF ST. MAWGAN
Newquay, Cornwall. *Military and civil flying and static display.*
📞 01637 872201

PAIGNTON REGATTA
Paignton Seafront, Devon. *Sailing, swimming, rowing and mammoth fair.*
📞 01803 555738

TREGONY HEAVY HORSE SHOW
Tregony, Truro, Cornwall. *Heavy horse display, trade stands.*
📞 01872 530357

DARTMOUTH ROYAL REGATTA
Dartmouth, Devon. *Various water-borne and land-based events, displays.*
📞 01803 832435

SEPTEMBER
COLYTON CARNIVAL
Colyton, Devon. *Week of fund-raising events, culminating in street carnival.*
📞 01297 553699

OCTOBER
EXETER CARNIVAL
Exeter, Devon. *Largest carnival procession in the West Country.*
📞 01392 76619

REGIONAL SHOPPING

All of the larger towns, and most of the smaller ones, have an excellent selection of shops to suit all tastes, including the main high street chains. To make your stay in the West Country just that little bit more memorable, however, we have selected a range of specialist shops that cater for the more discerning, with an eye for the unusual. Happy hunting!

ART & CRAFT SHOPS

The West Country has a rich tradition of crafts. Below is a small selection of shops where you will find many interesting and unusual items made by local craftspeople.

BOSCASTLE
Old Mill Craft Centre
The Bridge
☎ 01840 250230

BUCKLAND-IN-THE-MOOR
The Roundhouse Craft Centre
Southbrook Farm
☎ 01364 653234

EXETER
Arboretum Crafts
Harlequins Shopping Centre,
Paul Street
☎ 01392 494050

GORRAN HAVEN
Quayside Crafts
The Quay
☎ 01392 214332

The Old Customs House
☎ 01726 843055

HONITON
Pottery Shop & Craft Centre
30 High Street
☎ 01404 42106

PERRANPOTH
Spinners Web
9 Fore Street
☎ 01208 873037

ST. IVES
Bohemia
40 Foe Street
☎ 01736 796292

The Courtyard Shopping Mews
9 High Street
☎ 01736 793628

TINTAGEL
Avalon Craft Shop
Tremorrab,
Bossiney Road
☎ 01840 770415

TOTNES
Nick Agar Wood Turning
Cider Press Gate,
Skinners Bridge,
Dartington
☎ 01803 862277

GIFT SHOPS

The following is a small selection of gift shops offering exclusive items for those seeking something a little different, from ethnic jewellery and clothes to fine glass and china.

BOSCASTLE
National Trust Gift Shop,
Boscastle Harbour
☎ 01840 250353
(Unusual & quality gifts)

EXETER
The Blue Boy
22-24 Pincessshay
☎ 01392 258013
(Fine china and porcelain)

MEVAGISSEY
Cornish Goodies
West Wharf
☎ 01726 842086
(Unusual gifts)

OKEHAMPTON
Ethnix
7 The Arcade, Fore Street
☎ 01837 53062
(Clothes and gifts from the East)

PLYMPTON
Ideas
Colebrook Road, Colebrook
☎ 01752 348188
(Ceramics, lace, cards, dried flowers)

TINTAGEL
XIV Century Giftshop
Fore Street

TIVERTON
Tiverton China & Glass
123 Bampton Street

TORQUAY
James Rodney of Wellswood
17 Ilsham Road, Wellswood, Torquay
(Gifts, T-shirt design and printing)

LEATHERGOODS

Exclusive leather goods and craft.

EXETER
Cummings
34 Princesshay
📞 01392 273886

FALMOUTH
Cornish Sheepskin Shops
2 Portham House,
New Street
📞 01326 312242

ST. IVES
Leathercraft
62a Fore Street
📞 01736 793181

SHOPPING CENTRES

The following shopping centres and malls provide all-weather shopping.

BARNSTAPLE
Green Leaf Shopping Centre
📞 01271 322278

EXETER
Guildhall Shopping Centre
📞 01392 201910

PLYMOUTH
The Armada Shopping Centre
Armada Way
📞 01752 269471

SIDMOUTH
Sidmouth Shopping Centre
High Street
📞 01395 513652

TORQUAY
Fleet Walk Shopping Centre
Fleet Street
📞 01803 200508

Union Square Shopping Centre
📞 01803 294892

Also at Barnstaple is Butchers' Row, an entire street of small and quaint shops beneath an overhanging canopy.

MARKETS

Markets are always fun to explore for bargains or unusual gifts. The following have been carefully selected for their overall interest value.

BIDEFORD
Pannier Market
Market Place
📞 01237 478777
(Tues. & Sat.)

BRIXHAM
Pannier Market
New Road
📞 01803 851204
(Tues. & Fri.)

CAMBORNE
Indoor Market
Rosewarne Road
📞 01209 716117
(Every day except Sun.)

LOOE
Indoor Market
Bridgend, W. Looe
📞 01503 264895
(Every day)

NEWQUAY
Whitegate Market
Henver Road
📞 01637 874978
(Every day except Sun.)

NEWTON ABBOT
Corn Exchange
Market Street
📞 01626 353567
(Indoor Market - Mon.-Sat.)
(Outdoor Market - Wed. & Sat.)

OTTERY ST. MARY
Potters Country Market
West Hill Road
📞 01404 812825
(Every day)

PENZANCE
Bateman's Market
Causewayhead
📞 01736 363348
(Every day except Sun.)

REDRUTH
Indoor Market
Higher Fore Street
📞 01209 216186
(Every day except Sun.)

ST. MARYCHURCH
Indoor Market
Fore Street
📞 01803 316590
(Every day)

TRURO
Pannier Market
Lemon Quay
📞 01872 272490
(Mon.-Sat.)

ANTIQUES

Collectors items and curios.

EXETER
Westgate Curios
4 West Street
📞 01392 413396

PLYMOUTH
Old Curiosity Shop
The House that Jack Built,
Southside Street, The Barbican
📞 01752 224114

SOUTH MOLTON
The Dragon
8 George Arcade, Broad Street
📞 01769 572374

ST. IVES
Courtyard Collectables
Cyril Noall Square,
Fore Street
📞 01736 798809

WADEBRIDGE
Little Bridge Curios
Hamilton House, The Platt.

GENERAL INFORMATION

The following information is provided to assist visitors in making their stay in the West Country as trouble-free as possible.

WINING AND DINING

The choice of eating establishments in the West Country is limitless. Every town and most villages (especially on the coast) boast a range of pubs, cafés and restaurants, many specialising in delicious seafoods, and you are recommended to seek these out for yourself. For that special occasion, however, the following list of restaurants (recommended by the West Country Tourist Board) have been singled out for special mention because of the excellence and good value of their cuisine.

DEVON

The Arundel Arms
Lifton
☎ 01566 784666
(Former coaching inn on Cornish border. Excellent local fare, including Devon beef, Cornish salmon and sea bass.)

The Carved Angel
2 South Embankment,
Dartmouth
☎ 01803 832465
(Excellent restaurant overlooking River Dart. Also, licensed café serving lunch and afternoon teas.)

Chez Nous
13 Frankfort Gate,
Plymouth
☎ 01752 266793
(Close to Theatre Royal. Excellent menu, specialising in local produce, especially fish.)

The Drewe Arms
Broadhembury
☎ 01404 8412670
(Garden, bars, fresh fish and seafood a speciality; locally brewed beers.)

Gridleigh Park
Chagford
☎ 01647 432367
(Restaurant of international reputation, voted as one of the top ten in Britain.)

The Horn of Plenty
Gulworthy,
Tavistock
☎ 01822 832528
(Much celebrated and awarded cuisine. Restaurant set in family home.)

Hunts Tor Restaurant
Drewsteignton
☎ 01647 281228
(Historic house in picturesque postcard Dartmoor village. Set menu changed daily.)

Mote Chase Hotel & Restaurant
Nr. Ashburton
☎ 01364 631471
(11th-century hunting lodge set in parkland. Traditional English cuisine, using local produce.)

Percy's at Coombeshead
Virginstow, Nr. Launceston
☎ 01409 211236
(Vegetarian and special diets. Organic home-reared pork and duck, unusual salads, fresh seafood.)

Pophams
Castle Street, Winkleigh
☎ 01837 83767
(Informal restaurant of renown. Unlicensed, but bring your own.)

St. Olaves Court Hotel
Mary Archer Street, Exeter
☎ 01392 217736
(Candlelit restaurant specialising in West Country fare.)

Whitechapel Manor
Nr. South Molton
☎ 01769 573377
(Magnificent Elizabethan manor house; specialises in Devon produce.)

Woodhayes Hotel & Restaurant
Whimple, Nr. Exeter
☎ 01404 822237
(Georgian house, set six-course menu, changed daily.)

CORNWALL

The Cornish Cottage Hotel
New Polzeath, Nr. Rock
☎ 01208 862213

Jamaica Inn
Bolventor,
Near Bodmin
☎ 01566 86250
(Excellent bar food and full restaurant facilities in unique location - see page 30)

Pennypots Restaurant
Maenporth Beach,
Falmouth
☎ 01326 250251
(Informal, with stunning views of Falmouth Bay. Fixed price menu offering best of local produce.)

The Seafood Restaurant
Riverside, Padstow
☎ 01842 532485
(Delightful location on quayside. Seafood is bright, colourful, varied and cooked with imagination.)

The Well House
St. Keyne,
Liskeard
☎ 01579 342001
(Delightful house in valley. Local produce a speciality.)

WHERE TO DRINK

Britain is famed for the number and variety of its inns and pubs. Increasingly, more and more pubs offer a range of services and facilities, including accommodation, entertainment and meals to suit all tastes. The list is endless and you are recommended to find your own favourites. The St. Austell Brewery of Cornwall services over 150 pubs and inns throughout the West Country, specialising in traditional and local ales. For a complete list of locations ☎ 01726 66022.

NIGHTCLUBS CORNWALL

BUDE
Sandals Headlands
Crooklets Road
☎ 01288 352555

FALMOUTH
Paradox
The Moor
☎ 01326 314453

LAUNCESTON
Oasis Nightclub
Pannygillam Way
☎ 01566 776527

LISKEARD
The Carlton Suite
The Parade
☎ 01579 342731

NEWQUAY
Steamers
Moras Hill
☎ 01637 872194

Tall Trees Club
Tolcarne Road
☎ 01637 850313

PENZANCE
The Barn
Eastern Green
☎ 01736 365754

The Venue
Branwell's Mill,
Market Jew Street
☎ 01736 331211

Zero Club
Abbey Hill
☎ 01736 330680

REDRUTH
The Twilight Zone
Vauxhall
☎ 01209 215455

ST. IVES
Master Robert's Nightclub
Street An Pol
☎ 01736 796042

Mr. Peggottys
Porthmeor Road
☎ 01736 796011

TRURO
The Eclipse Nightclub
16 St. Mary's Street
☎ 01872 241706

The Loft Club
Lemon Quay
☎ 01872 261199

NIGHTCLUBS DEVON

BARNSTAPLE
Bees Nightclub & Discotheque
☎ 01271 373393

BIDEFORD
Caesar's Palace
King Street
☎ 01237 478022

Cleopatra's
13 Honestone Street
☎ 01237 424440

EXETER
The Carver Club
83-84 Queen Street
☎ 01392 495370

Club Rococo
Mary Archer Street
☎ 01392 434411

Humphrey B's
81 Fore Street
☎ 01392 422221

The Warehouse & Boxer
376 Commercial Road
☎ 01392 259292

ILFRACOMBE
Lucky's Nightclub
11-12 High Street
☎ 01271 866667

EXMOUTH
The Q Club
Manchester Street
☎ 01395 265333

HONITON
The Paradise Club
Northcote Lane
☎ 01404 43159

KINGSBRIDGE
Fusion Nightclub
Union Road
☎ 01548 857021

TORQUAY
Claire's Club
41 Torwood Street
☎ 01803 292079

Club Rio
Victoria Park
☎ 01803 295078

The Ibiza Bar
3 Victoria Parade
☎ 01803 214334

The Monastery Nightclub
Torwood Gardens Road
☎ 01803 297929

Monroes Nightclub
Victoria Road
☎ 01803 291149

OKEHAMPTON
Neros 92
4 Market Street
☎ 01837 53888

PLYMOUTH
Anza Leisure
The Parade
☎ 01752 224144

Blondz Nightclub
Union Street
☎ 01752 266118

Dance Academy
121-123 Union Street
☎ 01752 220055

Images Club & Wine Bar
89a Cornwall Street
☎ 01752 660815

Gates Fun Pub
Union Street
☎ 01752 662100

Zero's
24 Lockyer Street
☎ 01752 662346

Zoom
48 Union Street
☎ 01752 256404

The Verve
13 Torwood Street
☎ 01803 212903

SEATON
The Grove
Fore Street
☎ 01297 21077

SIDMOUTH
New Tavern & Carinas
Fore Street &
Market Street
☎ 01395 514692

WOOLACOMBE
Marisco Club
Barton Road
☎ 01271 870960

THEATRES CORNWALL

FALMOUTH
Falmouth Arts Centre
Church Street
☎ 01326 212300

Princess Pavilion
Melvill Road
☎ 01326 211222

LISKEARD
Sterts Arts & Environmental Centre
Upton Cross
☎ 01579 362382

NEWQUAY
Jesters Theatre Club
Pentire Hotel
☎ 01637 851186

PORTHCURNO
Minack Theatre
☎ 01736 810181

GENERAL INFORMATION

REDRUTH
Regal Theatre
Fore Street
☎ 01209 315161

ST. AUSTELL
Restormel Arts
High Cross Street
☎ 01726 68532

*St. Austell
Arts Centre*
Truro Road
☎ 01726 73949

TRURO
Hall for Cornwall
Back Quay
☎ 01872 262466

Redannick Theatre
Redannick Lane
☎ 01872 222272

THEATRES DEVON

BABBACOMBE
Babbacombe Theatre
Babbacombe Downs Road
☎ 01803 328385

BARNSTAPLE
*North Devon
Theatres Trust*
Boutport Street
☎ 01271 324242

BRIXHAM
Brixham Theatre
Bolton Cross
☎ 01803 852829

CREDITON
Drama Centre
East Street
☎ 01363 773260

DAWLISH
*Shaftesbury
Theatre*
Brunswick Place
☎ 01626 863061

EXETER
Barnfield Theatre
Barnfield Road
☎ 01392 271808

*Exeter & Devon
Arts Centre*
Bradrinch Place
☎ 01392 667080

EXMOUTH
Blackmore Theatre
Bicton Street
☎ 01395 276681

Pavilion
Esplanade
☎ 01395 22247

HOLSWORTHY
*Holsworthy
Theatre*
Bodmin Street
☎ 01409 253826

KINGSBRIDGE
*South Hams Theatre
& Arts Trust*
Town Hall, Fore Street
☎ 01584 856636

PAIGNTON
Festival Theatre
Esplanade
☎ 01803 290290

PLYMOUTH
Plymouth Pavlions
Millbay Road
☎ 01752 229922

Theatre Royal
Royal Parade
☎ 01752 267222

Plymouth Athenaeum
Demys Cross
☎ 01752 266104

SIDMOUTH
*Sidmouth Manor
Pavilion*
Manor Road
☎ 01395 514413

TAVISTOCK
*Wharf Community
Arts Centre*
☎ 01822 611166

TIVERTON
New Hall
Borrington Street
☎ 01884 253404

TORQUAY
The Little Theatre
St. Marks Road
☎ 01803 299330

TORRINGTON
Plough Arts Centre
Fore Street
☎ 01805 624624

TOTNES
Dartington Arts
The Gallery, Dartington Hall
☎ 01803 863073

CONCERT HALLS

CORNWALL
Coliseum
Carlyon Bay, Par
☎ 01726 814004

CINEMAS CORNWALL

PADSTOW
Capitol Cinema
Middle Street
☎ 01841 532344

PENZANCE
Savoy Cinema
Causewayhead
☎ 01736 363330

REDRUTH
Regal Cinema
Fore Street
☎ 01209 216278

ST. AUSTELL
Filmcentre
Chandos Place
☎ 01726 73750

ST. IVES
Royal Cinema
Chapel Street
☎ 01736 796843

TRURO
The Plaza
Lemon Street
☎ 01872 272894

WADEBRIDGE
Regal Cinema
The Platt
☎ 01208 812791

CINEMAS DEVON

BARNSTAPLE
Astor Cinema
Bortport Street
☎ 01271 342550

EXETER
Exeter Picture House
Bartholomew Street West
☎ 01392 435522

Odeon
Sidwell Street
☎ 08705 050007

EXMOUTH
Savoy Film Centre
Rolle Street
☎ 01395 268220

ILFRACOMBE
*Pendle Stairway
Cinema*
High Street
☎ 01271 863484

NEWTON ABBOT
Alexandra Cinema
Market Street
☎ 01626 365368

OKEHAMPTON
Carlton Cinema
St. James Street
☎ 01837 52167

PAIGNTON
Torbay Picture House
Torbay Road
☎ 012803 559544

PLYMOUTH
ABC
Derrys Cross
☎ 01752 225553

Drake Odeon
Derrys Cross
☎ 01752 668825

SIDMOUTH
Radway Cinema
Radway Place
☎ 01395 513085

TEIGNMOUTH
Riviera Cinema
Den Crescent
☎ 01626 774624

TIVERTON
Tivoli Cinema
Fore Street
☎ 01884 252157

TORQUAY
Odeon
Abbey Road
☎ 01803 292324

WIDEMOUTH BAY
Rebel Cinema
Poundstook
☎ 01288 361442

TOURIST INFORMATION CENTRES

West Country Tourist Board
60 St. David's Hill,
Exeter, Devon
☎ 01392 276351
📠 01392 420891
E-mail: post@wctb.co.uk
Internet:http://www.wctb.co.uk

CORNWALL

BODMIN
Shire House, Mount Folly Square, PL31 2DQ
☎ 01208 76616

BUDE
Visitor Centre,
The Crescent, EX23 8LE
☎ 01288 354240

CAMELFORD
North Cornwall Museum,
The Clease, PL32 9PL
☎ 01840 212954
(Seasonal)

FALMOUTH
28 Killigrew Street,
TR11 3PN
☎ 01326 312300

FOWEY
4 Custom House Hill,
PL23 1AB
☎ 01726 833616

HELSTON & LIZARD PENINSULA
79 Meneage Street,
Helston, TR13 8RB
☎ 01326 565431

LAUNCESTON
Market House Arcade,
Market Street, PL15 8EP
☎ 01566 772321

LOOE
The Guildhall, PL13 1AA
☎ 01503 262072
(Seasonal)

NEWQUAY
Municipal Office,
Marcus Hill, TR7 1BD
☎ 01637 871345

PADSTOW
Red Brick Building,
North Quay,
PL28 8AF
☎ 01841 533449

PENZANCE
Station Road, TR18 2NF
☎ 01736 362207

ISLES OF SCILLY
Porthcressa Bank,
St.Mary's, TR21 0JL
☎ 01720 422536

ST. IVES
The Guildhall,
Street an Pol, TR26 2DS
☎ 01736 796297

TRURO
Municipal Building,
Boscawen Street, TR1 2NE
☎ 01872 274555

WADEBRIDGE
The Town Hall,
The Platt, PL27 7EG
☎ 01208 813725

DEVON

AXMINSTER
The Old Courthouse,
Church Street,
EX13 5AQ
☎ 01297 34386
(Seasonal)

BARNSTAPLE
36 Boutport Street,
EX31 1RX
☎ 01271 375000

BIDEFORD
Victoria Park,
The Quay, EX39 2QQ
☎ 01237 477676

BRAUNTON
The Bakehouse Centre,
Caen Street, EX33 1AA
☎ 01271 816400

BRIXHAM
The Old Market House,
The Quay, TQ5 8TB
☎ 01803 852861

BUDLEIGH SALTERTON
Fore Street, EX9 6NG
☎ 01395 445275

COMBE MARTIN
Cross Street, EX34 0DH
☎ 01271 883319
(Seasonal)

CREDITON
Market Street Car Park,
Market Street, EX17 2BN
☎ 01363 772006
(Seasonal)

DARTMOUTH
The Engine House, Mayor's Avenue, TQ6 9YY
☎ 01803 834224

DAWLISH
The Lawn, EX7 9EL
☎ 01626 863589

DEVON SERVICES
Sidmouth Road, EX2 7HF.
☎ 01392 437581

EXETER
Civic Centre,
Paris Street, EX1 1RP
☎ 01392 265700

EXMOUTH
Alexandra Terrace,
EX8 1NZ
☎ 01395 222299

HONITON
Lace Walk Car Park,
EX14 8LT
☎ 01404 43716

ILFRACOMBE
The Promenade, EX34 9BX
☎ 01271 863001

IVYBRIDGE
South Dartmoor,
Tourist Centre,
Leonards Road, PL21 0SL
☎ 01752 897035

KINGSBRIDGE
The Quay, TQ7 1HS
☎ 01548 853195

LYNTON
Town Hall,
Lee Road EX35 6BT
☎ 01598 752225

MODBURY
Poundwell Meadow Car Park, PL21 0QL
☎ 01548 830195
(Seasonal)

NEWTON ABBOT
6 Bridge House,
Courtenay Street,
TQ12 4QS
☎ 01626 367494

OKEHAMPTON
3 West Street,
EX20 1HQ
☎ 01837 53020
(Seasonal)

OTTERY ST. MARY
10b Broad Street,
EX11 1BZ
☎ 01404 813964
(Seasonal)

PAIGNTON
The Esplanade, TQ4 6BN
☎ 01803 558383

PLYMOUTH
Island House,
9 The Barbican,
PL1 1LS
☎ 01752 264849

Plymouth Discovery Centre,
Crabtree, PL3 6RN
☎ 01752 266030

SALCOMBE
Council Hall,
Market Street, TQ8 8DE
☎ 01548 843927

SEATON
The Underfleet, EX12 2TB
☎ 01297 21660

SIDMOUTH
Ham Lane, EX10 8XR
☎ 01395 516441

SOUTH MOLTON
1 East Street, EX36 3BU
☎ 01769 574122
(Seasonal)

TAVISTOCK
Town Hall,
Bedford Square PL19 0AE
☎ 01822 612938

TEIGNMOUTH
The Den,
Sea Front TQ14 8BE
☎ 01626 779769

TIVERTON
Phoenix Lane, EX16 6LU
☎ 01884 255827

GENERAL INFORMATION

TORQUAY
Vaughan Parade,
TQ2 5JG
☎ 01803 297428

TOTNES
The Town Mill,
Coronation Road,
TQ9 5DF
☎ 01803 863168

WHIDDON DOWN
Little Chef,
Nr. Okehampton,
EX20 2QT
☎ 01647 231375

WOOLACOMBE
Red Barn Café Car Park,
Barton Road
☎ 01271 870553

USEFUL ADDRESSES

Cornwall Wildlife Trust
Five Acres, Allet, Truro
☎ 01872 73939

Dartmoor National Park
(General enquiries)
☎ 01626 832093

Devon Wildlife Trust
Shirehampton House,
35-37 St. David's Hill,
Exeter
☎ 01392 279244

English Heritage Historic
Properties South West,
7/8 King Street,
Bristol, BS1 4EQ
☎ 0117 9750700

Exmoor National Park
☎ 01598 752509
(General enquiries)

National Rivers Authority
Marley House,
Kestrel Way, Exeter
☎ 01392 444000

National Trust for Cornwall
Cornwall Regional Office,
Lanhydrock, Bodmin
☎ 01208 74281

National Trust for Devon
Killerton House,
Broadclyst, Exeter
☎ 01392 881691

ACCOMMODATION

Because of the rich diversity of accommodation available in Britain, ranging from simple camping and caravan sites and holiday camps to bed and breakfast establishments, guest houses and a wide range of hotels of all classes, it is generally assumed that individuals will want to book their accommodation themselves beforehand. Tourist Information Centres (on pages 42-44) offer extensive lists of locally available accommodation and many operate a book-a-bed-ahead scheme for travellers.

HOW TO GET THERE

ROAD LINKS
The West Country is not well served by motorway links, having only a short stretch of the M5, which terminates at Exeter.
The M5 connects with the M4, however, allowing for good connections to London, the M25 and most other regions of the country.
There is a good network of 'A' roads, including the A30/A303 which connects Land's End to the M3 and M25. Several long sections of 'A' road have been designated Primary Routes and have been made into dual carriageways.

RAIL LINKS
Until recently, all of Britain's rail network came under the auspices of the nationalised British Rail, but this has now been broken up into several individual private companies. It is not always necessary to break long journeys when crossing between regions, but each company has a slightly different operating procedure. If in doubt, check at local stations. There is a direct rail link from London, Paddington, to Penzance and Exeter. A fast network of Inter-City trains also connects the main towns of the West Country to all other regions of Britain.

National Rail enquiries
☎ 0345 484950

Rail Ticket Sales
☎ 0345 125625

AIRPORTS
There are two regional airports in Devon, at Plymouth and Exeter, and one at Newquay, in Cornwall.

Each offers connecting flights to other regions and international airports, such as London and Cardiff. There is a heliport at Penzance, in Cornwall, offering regular connecting flights to the Isles of Scilly.

Newquay Airport Enquiries
☎ 1091 2860966

Exeter Airport Enquiries
☎ 01392 367433

Plymouth Airport Enquiries
☎ 01752 772752

Penzance Heliport Enquiries
☎ 01736 363871

PUBLIC TRANSPORT
Public transport in the Southwest is good locally, but most services operate within a limited catchment area, with few links between towns. Some services only operate on a seasonal basis. For general information on public transport (buses) contact:

Public Transport Information
☎ 01392 382800

For local timetable information contact the relevant Tourist Information Centre in the first instance. They should be able to give you the contact number for local bus operatives. For information for travellers with disabilities, contact:

Travel Enquiries (Disabled)
☎ 01392 382123

COACH OPERATORS
Britain has several extensive networks of privately-run coach companies that run regular services to the main towns of the West Country and to all other regions.

First Western National
☎ 01752 222666

National Express Coach Services
☎ 0990 808080

EXCURSIONS
Several coach companies also run excursions to places of interest throughout the region. Check with your hotel or local tour operator, or contact the nearest Tourist Information Centre for details. First Western National (see above) also run excursions.

FERRIES
International ferries operate out of Plymouth to Santander in Spain and Roscoff in France. A regular ferry service also operates between Penzance and the Isles of Scilly. Several local ferries operate across river estuaries and a regular service runs between Ilfracombe and Bideford to Lundy Island.

CAR RENTAL
All of the major car rental companies operate in the Southwest, but there are many local companies too, offering competitive rates. You are advised to shop around.

MORE INFORMATION

REGIONAL NEWSPAPERS

Local newspapers and periodicals which may be of interest to the visitor include: *Cornish & Devon Post, Cornish Guardian, Cornish Times* and *Western Morning News*. These are all widely available at newsagents and can be used to provide up-to-the-minute information.

A Talking News for the Blind service is available on:

📞 01822 618922

LOCAL RADIO & TELEVISION

TELEVISION

The local television station for this region is West Country Television.

RADIO

The region is covered by three local radio stations, including B.B.C. Radio Cornwall (103.9 FM); B.B.C. Radio Devon (103.4 FM) and Plymouth Sounds Radio (97 FM/1152 AM).

OVERSEAS VISITORS

DRIVING

Always ensure that you have the necessary driving permits and insurance before driving in the U.K. Drive on the left side of the road, and at roundabouts give way to the right, unless otherwise instructed. Signposting is generally very good, but you should purchase a copy of the Highway Code for clarification. Road surfaces are generally excellent. Use designated car parks whenever possible and never park on double yellow lines on the road edge.

HEALTH CARE

Before travelling to the U.K. you should ensure that you have been suitably inoculated (according to your country of origin). There are no prevalent infectious diseases in the U.K. and no vaccinations are required. The water is safe to drink straight from the tap. Whilst here, you will be entitled to free health care at National Health Service hospitals, although some, or all, of the cost may be recharged to you if your country of origin does not have a reciprocal arrangement with the U.K.. Please note that dental and eye care is not free.

VAT REFUNDS

Foreign visitors can apply for a refund of VAT for purchases over £50 - ask for a form when making your purchase.

ELECTRICITY

The electricity supply in Britain uses 240 volts AC. Plug adapters are available in most electrical appliance stores.

TIPPING

There is no formal system for tipping in Britain, as in some other countries, and it still remains a highly debatable issue. Generally, a tip of about 10% is acceptable at restaurants, hairdressers and for taxi drivers. Hotel porters might expect a £1 coin tip.

Elsewhere, tipping is not generally expected, though, of course, this is up to the individual.

WALKING & CYCLING

GETTING OUT & ABOUT

One of the finest ways to explore any region is to use the Public Rights of Way that criss-cross every part of this country. Britain possesses a unique network of some 120,000 miles (193,080 km) of public footpaths, bridleways and byways, most crossing private land.

This fascinating network of paths was not created in recent ages for recreational purposes, but is rooted firmly in history, some perhaps being as much as 4,000 years old. They formed part of the highways network

in the past, used by villagers to get to work or church, or by traders carrying their wares. They are still maintained as highways by local authorities and are protected in law. Often located in beautiful, remote countryside, there is no better way to see Britain.

WHAT TO TAKE

The pull-out walks and cycle rides in this guide have been specially devised so that they are suitable even for the inexperienced. It is usually best to *travel as light as possible*, but always wear appropriate footwear and clothing. Although those places selected here have at least some facilities, it is usually best to assume that none will be available. You should plan your itinerary accordingly and take essential supplies and refreshments with you in case, for any reason, they are not available on the route.

Remember to tell someone where you are planning to go, in case of an accident. Although some may prefer the solace of lone walking or cycling, it is usually better to take at least one companion (or a mobile phone) in case of emergency. Additionally, you should always take the relevant O.S. Pathfinder or Explorer map.

KNOW YOUR RIGHTS

Although the Local Highways Authority is responsible for maintaining Public Rights of Way, it rarely owns the land over which the paths run. Landowners, therefore, can claim a greater right of use and are permitted to plough cross-field paths, provided they are reinstated within two weeks, though headland paths should never be ploughed. It is illegal to obstruct a path or otherwise prevent someone from using it and all irregularities should be reported to the local highways authority. Paths can be legally diverted or stopped-up, however, though notices must be posted and new routes waymarked.

A map showing all Public Rights of Way is maintained by the relevant Highways Authority and can usually be consulted at any reasonable time. The routes shown in this guide were accurate at the time of going to press, but things can change. If you are in any doubt about your rights, or the routes, contact the relevant highways authority.

For Walks 1 and 2 and Cycle Ride 2, contact:

Cornwall County Council
📞 01872 322000

For Walk 3 and Cycle Ride 1, contact:

Devon County Council
📞 01392 382000

When using the Public Rights of Way network, please always show care and consideration for landowners and people living in the locality (especially when parking) and follow the Country Code at all times.

GENERAL INFORMATION

ADDITIONAL INFORMATION FOR SAFE CYCLING

Always ensure that your bicycle is in good working order and that it is the correct size. Take great care on the roads, especially with right turns; if necessary, dismount and cross the road on foot. When out riding it is essential to wear bright clothing, carry lights and take waterproofs. Always carry refreshments, a small tool kit, puncture repair kit, first-aid kit and enough money for emergencies. It is important to stay alert at all times; be ready for pedestrians on narrow lanes and fast traffic on main roads. Finally, always follow the advice contained in the Highway Code.

THE COUNTRY CODE

- Enjoy the countryside and respect its life and work.
- Guard against all risk of fire.
- Leave all gates as you find them.
- Keep all dogs under close control.
- Keep to public paths across farmland.
- Use gates and stiles to cross fences, hedges and walls.
- Leave livestock, crops and machinery alone.
- Take your litter home.
- Help to keep all water clean.
- Protect wildlife, plants and trees.
- Take special care on country roads.
- Make no unnecessary noise.

MONEY MATTERS

BANKS

The list of banks and building societies throughout the West Country would be too lengthy to include here. Most of the larger towns throughout the region will have branches of these insitutions, including the four main banks (Barclays, Midland, National Westminster and Lloyds), at most of the main towns throughout the region. In case of emergencies, Tourist Information Centres will be able to give you a complete list of branches of all banks or building societies.

BUREAU DE CHANGE

Thomas Cook Ltd
38 High Street, Exeter
☎ 01392 425712

17 Boscawen Street, Truro
☎ 01872 241238

4 Old Town Street, Plymouth
(Within Midland Bank)
☎ 01752 603610

Most main branches of banks and building societies also operate a foreign money exchange service, please check with individual branches for details. Travellers' cheques and Eurocheques are also widely accepted at shops and restaurants.

CREDIT CARDS

All major credit and debit cards are accepted throughout Britain, including Visa, Mastercard, American Express, Diners, Switch and Delta.

WHEN THINGS GO WRONG

IF YOU ARE UNWELL

For routine accidents or health problems, contact the local hospital of the region you are staying in. Local doctors will also usually see visitors - contact your nearest Tourist Information Centre for details (see page 43) or ask at your hotel or a chemist shop. General information on N.H.S. services and treatments is available from:

National Health Service
☎ 0800 665544

EMERGENCIES

In the case of genuine emergencies only dial 999, free of charge. Speak slowly and clearly and give the operator details of which service you require: Ambulance, Police, Fire Brigade or Coastguard.

LIFEGUARDS

Several local authorities now provide Lifeguard services at beaches within their control. If you see someone in difficulty in the water, always contact the lifeguard where possible rather than attempt a rescue yourself.

POLICE

For all non-urgent police matters, you should contact:

Devon and Cornwall Constabulary Force (24 hrs)
☎ 0990 700400

INDEX

A
accommodation 44
adventure activities 14-17, 36-37
aircraft 15, 37
animals 8-12, 16, 17, 20, 36-7
art 4, 9, 28-31
Arthur, King 14, 22-3, 25
Axe, river 31

B
balloon trips 16
Barnstaple 10, 39
beaches 4-7
Becky Falls 21
Bedruthan Steps 5
Beer 7, 11
Berry Pomeroy Castle 22
Bicton Horse Trials 36
Bideford 10, 39
The Big Sheep 10
Bigbury-on-Sea 6
birdwatching 6, 16
Blackpool Sands 7
boat trips 7, 15, 36
Bodmin 14, 18, 24, 29, 32
Bolventor 30
Boscastle 31, 38
Brixham 12, 31, 35, 37, 39
Brunel, I.K. 3
Buckland Abbey 23, 27
Bude 14, 37
Burgh Island 6
Bygones, Torquay 11

C
Callestock Cider Farm 8
Calstock 28
Camborne 3, 36, 39
Carrick Roads 19, 25
Cascades Family Adventure Pool 17
castles 16, 21-7, 34
cathedrals 26, 32, 35
caves 5, 12, 23
Chapel Porth 9, 14
Charlestown 31
Cheesewring 18, 20
children 5, 8-11, 13
cider 8, 27
climate 2, 4, 28, 33, 35
Clovelly 20
Clyst St Mary 36, 38
Coastguard 6, 46
Colyton 31, 36, 37
Combe Martin 10
Compton Castle 27
Cornish language 25
Cotehele House 28-9
Croyde Bay 17
Culdrose 9, 15, 37
Cullompton 36
cycling 45-6

D
Dart, river 34
Dartington Crystal 11
Dartmoor 3, 16, 17, 21, 34
Dartmouth 27, 34, 37
Devonport 16
Dobwall's Theme Park 9
Donkey Sanctuary 8
Drake, Sir Francis 23, 27, 35
drystone walls 19

E
East Budleigh 36
emergencies 6, 46
entertainment 41-2
events 36-7
Exeter 13, 26, 35-9
Exmoor 10, 17, 20
Exmouth 7, 36

F
Falmouth 15, 19, 25, 33, 39
farms 8, 10, 26
festivals 36-7
fishing 2, 4, 7, 15, 19, 37

Flambards 9, 36
food 13, 30, 33, 35
Fowey 15, 18, 36, 37

G
gardens 2, 6, 9-11, 19, 23-4, 28-9
geology 3
Gerrans Bay 19
Golitha Falls 18
Gorran Haven 5, 37
Grenville, Sir Richard 27
Gweek 9

H
Hallsands 16
Hartland 29, 30
Helford 19
Helston 9, 36
Holsworthy 37
Honiton 38, 39
Hurlers 18

I
Ilfracombe 16
industry 2, 3, 11, 13, 14, 36
information 40-6
Instow 28
Isles of Scilly 15, 23, 33, 36

J
Jamaica Inn Museums 30
Jekyll, Gertrude 29

K
Kent's Cavern 12, 31
Kingsbridge 17, 26
Kynance Cove 5

L
Land's End 4, 15
Lanyon Quoit 22
Launceston 24
legends 5, 22-3, 25
Liskeard 9
Lizard Peninsula 4
Looe 8, 15, 39
Lostwithiel 24
Lundy Island 16

Lustleigh 21
Lydford 21
Lynmouth 20
Lynton 20

M
Man-an-tol stone 22
Manaton 21
Marazion 25
Marham 37
marine life 12
Merlin's Cave 23
Mevagissey 12, 15, 19, 38
Minack Theatre 4, 18
mining 3, 9, 13, 14
Minions 18
Monkey Sanctuary 8
Morwellam Quay 13
Mount Edgcumbe 29
Mount's Bay 25, 33
Mullion 4
Murrayton 8
museums 8, 24, 29-34

N
Newquay 4, 12, 14, 15, 24, 37, 39
Newton Abbot 39
Noss Mayo 21

O
Okehampton 38
Ottery St Mary 39

P
Paignton 11, 22, 35, 37
Pecorama, Beer 11
Pencarrow House 29
Pendennis Castle 25
Pendower 5, 19
Penhallow 8
Penwith Peninsula 30
Penzance 15, 22, 33, 39
Perranporth 38
Plymouth 21, 23, 27, 35, 37, 39
Plympton 38
Poldark Mine 13
Polperro 19
Polurrian Cove 4

INDEX & ACKNOWLEDGMENTS

ponies 8, 16, 17
Porthcurno 4, 18
Porthmeor 30
Powderham 26, 37

R
railways 7, 9-12, 14, 20, 24
Redruth 39
Restormel Castle 24
Roche 22
Roseland 19
Royal Navy 34

S
St Agnes 3, 9, 14, 38
St Austell 13
St Cleer 18
St George's Island 15
St Ives 4, 14, 30, 36, 38, 39
St Mawes Castle 25
St Michael's Mount 25
Salcombe 6, 21
Saltash 3
Sealife Centre 12

seals 9
Seaton 31
serpentine 5
Sharpitor 6
Shipwreck & Heritage Centre 31
shipwrecks 5, 23, 31
shopping 38-9
Sidmouth 39
Slapton 6
smuggling 4, 7, 30
Soar Mill Cove 6
South Molton 39
standing stones 18, 22
surfing 4, 6

T
Tamar Otter Park 24
Tamar, river 3, 13, 28
Tapeley Park Gardens 28
Tate Gallery, St Ives 30
Tavistock 13, 23, 39
Teignmouth 39
Tintagel 23, 25, 38

Tiverton 38
Torquay 11-12, 28, 31, 35-9
Torre Abbey 28
Totnes 27, 34, 38
Tourist Information Centres 42-44
Tramway Museum 31
travel 44
Tregony 37
Trerice 24
Trethevy Quoit 18
Trevithick, Richard 3, 36
Truro 26, 32, 39

U
Underground Tunnels 13, 35

V
Valley of the Rocks 20
Veryan 19
villages 19-21

W
Wadebridge 8, 37, 39
walking 6, 45-6

water sports 14, 17, 36-7
see also surfing
waterfalls 10, 18, 21
Wendron 13
Westward Ho! 38
Wheal Coates 3, 14
White Lady Waterfall 21
wildlife 9, 10, 12, 16
Wildlife & Dinosaur Park 10
windsurfing 14
wining & dining 40
witches 31, 37
Woolacombe 7
World of Model Railways 12
wreckers 5, 23

Y
yachting 33, 37
Yarde Farmhouse 26
Yealm, river 21

Z
Zoo, Paignton 11

ACKNOWLEDGEMENTS

We would like to thank: John Guy, Elaine Wilkinson, David Hobbs, Sue Lightfoot and Elizabeth Wiggans for their assistance.

Copyright © 1999 ticktock Publishing Ltd.

First published in Great Britain by ticktock Publishing Ltd., The Offices in the Square, Hadlow, Tonbridge, Kent TN11 0DD, Great Britain. All rights reserved.

No part of this publication may be reproduced, stored in a retrieval system, or transmitted in any form or by any means electronic, mechanical, photocopying, recording or otherwise, without prior written permission of the copyright owner.

A CIP catalogue record for this book is available from the British Library. ISBN 1 86007 133 3

Picture research by Image Select. Printed in Hong Kong.

Picture Credits: t=top, b=bottom, c=centre, l=left, r=right

Ann Ronan; 22bl. David Sellman; IFC. Dr. Thomas Hagen; 29cl. Greg Evans; 17cl, 20cr. J. Allan Cash; OFC & 13tr, 23cl, 32cr, 33cr. National Maritime Museum; 27br. Peter Cooper; 14tl, 45br, 15bl, 17bl. Philip Jarrett; 17b, 37c. Spectrum Colour Library; OFC main pic & 6tl, OFC, OFC & 16t, 4tl, 7ctr, 15br, OFC & 20tl, 35tl, 40tl. West Devon Borough Council; 23tr.

Some of the additional images were supplied digitally by Corel Ltd. The pull-out walks and cycle routes were kindly verified by Head of Communications at the Dartmoor National Park, and the Countryside Access Manager, Transportation & Estates Department at Cornwall County Council.

Every effort hass been made to ensure that the information in this book is as up to date as possible at the time of going to press. However, details such as telephone numbers, opening hours, prices and travel information are liable to change. The publishers cannot accept responsibility for any consequence arising from the use of this book.

Please send any corrections and suggestions for improvement in the next edition to. HMTE ticktock Publishing. The Offices in the Square, Hadlow, Tonbridge, Kent. TN11 0DD